P9-EAN-840

DATE DUE

JE 6 00			
DE 1 9 00			
AR 12 02			
AR 8 02			
AR 2 05			

Logistics
and Retail
Management

INSIGHTS INTO
CURRENT PRACTICE
AND TRENDS FROM
LEADING EXPERTS

Edited by
John Fernie
and
Leigh Sparks

CRC Press
Boca Raton   London   New York   Washington, D.C.

KOGAN
PAGE

YOURS TO HAVE AND TO HOLD
BUT NOT TO COPY

First published in 1999

Apart from any fair dealing for the purposes of research or private study, or criticism or review, as permitted under the Copyright, Designs and Patents Act, 1988, this publication may only be reproduced, stored or transmitted, in any form or by any means, with the prior permission in writing of the publishers, or in the case of reprographic reproduction in accordance with the terms and licences issued by the CLA. Enquiries concerning reproduction outside those terms should be sent to the publishers at the undermentioned address:

Kogan Page Limited
120 Pentonville Road
London N1 9JN
UK

CRC Press
Rights and Permissions
2000 NW Corporate Blvd
Boca Raton
Florida 3343
USA

© John Fernie and Leigh Sparks 1999

The right of John Fernie and Leigh Sparks to be identified as the author of this work has been asserted by them in accordance with the Copyright, Designs and Patents Act 1988.

British Library Cataloguing in Publication Data

A CIP record for this book is available from the British Library.

ISBN 0 7494 2834 1

Library of Congress Catalog Card Number 99-72247
ISBN 0 8493 4084 5

Typeset by Saxon Graphics Ltd, Derby
Printed and bound in Great Britain by Biddles Ltd, Guildford and King's Lynn

CONTENTS

CONTENTS

CONTRIBUTORS

Lawrence Christensen is Logistics Director, Safeway Stores plc. Born in South Shields in 1943, Lawrence started his career with the Merchant Navy, achieving the rank of 2nd Officer and with the Royal Navy as Lieutenant RNR. He left the Navy in 1968 and held management positions in the plastics industry and the shipbuilding industry. In 1974 he joined Cavenham Foods as distribution controller, which was later acquired by Argyll. Lawrence was appointed to the Board of Safeway as Logistics Director in 1991. He is chairman of the CIES Logistics Committee and has recently been appointed President of the Freight Transport Association. He is also a Fellow of the Institute of Management Services and a Fellow of the Institute of Logistics Management. He lives in Berkshire and is married with one son. His interests include riding, reading and keeping fit.

Martin G Christopher is Professor of Marketing and Logistics Systems at Cranfield School of Management, where he is Head of the Marketing and Logistics Faculty and Chairman of the Cranfield

Centre for Logistics and Transportation. In addition, he is Deputy Director of the School of Management responsible for Executive Development Programmes.

His interests in marketing and logistics strategy are reflected in his consultancy and management development activities. In this connection Martin Christopher has worked for major international companies in North America, Europe, the Far East and Australasia. He is also a non-executive director of a number of companies.

As an author, Martin has written numerous books and articles and is on the editorial advisory board of a number of professional journals in the marketing and logistics area. He is co-editor of the *International Journal of Logistics Management* and his recent books have focused upon Relationship Marketing, Customer Service and Logistics Strategy. He has held appointments as Visiting Professor at the University of British Columbia, Canada, the University of New South Wales, Australia and the University of South Florida, USA. He is a Fellow of the Chartered Institute of Marketing and of the Institute of Logistics Management, on whose Council he sits. In 1987 he was awarded the Sir Robert Lawrence medal of the Institute of Logistics and Distribution Management for his contribution to the development of logistics education in Britain.

John Fernie is Professor of Retailing and Logistics and Director of the Institute for Retail Studies at the University of Stirling. He has written and contributed to numerous textbooks in addition to publishing articles in academic journals and the trade press. His main research interests are in the field of retail management, especially in the areas of internationalization of retail formats and retail logistics. He also has undertaken a range of consultancy projects for a variety of retail and distribution companies. He was named editor of the year by MCB in 1997 for his contribution to the *International Journal of Retail & Distribution Management*. He is also an active member of both the Institute of Logistics, the Chartered Institute of Marketing and is an officer of the American Collegiate Retailing Association.

Paul Jackson is currently Senior Lecturer in International Business Studies, Coventry Business School, Coventry University. He has lectured for a number of years both internationally and within the United Kingdom on Retail, Logistics and Supply Chain Management.

For over 30 years Paul worked as a Senior Manager for Marks and Spencer. During this time he worked in a wide variety of roles, including General Management of some of Marks and Spencer's stores, Training and Development, Recruitment and Selection. For the last five years Paul was working as an IT and Logistics Project Manager implementing several major projects including the one described in his contribution to this book.

John O'Hagan is Divisional Managing Director of Hays Retail Support Services, the Hays company which pioneered non-merchandise logistics services in the UK. He is now looking to develop the concept throughout Europe. He has over 18 years' experience in logistics management. A former NFC graduate trainee, he held a number of management positions with the NFC and United Carriers before joining Hays in 1989.

Helen Peck is a researcher with the Marketing and Logistics Group at Cranfield. She is involved in the development of teaching material for graduate programmes and research and consultancy for corporate clients. Previously she worked with the School's management advisory service in the development of in-company programmes and in the library where she specialised in the retrieval and analysis of business information. She has travelled widely and published articles and papers on social, economic and political reform in Eastern Europe and China. Before joining the School in 1983, she worked for a major UK bank.

David Smith is Head of Primary Distribution at Tesco. After working in other sectors of high street retail distribution he joined Tesco in 1984 in the distribution division and worked in the fast-moving food consumer and temperature-controlled distribution networks in both secondary and primary distribution. In 1993 he completed an MBA at Stirling University with a dissertation on 'Integrated supply-chain management: the case of fresh produce in Tesco'. He has been recently involved with the Government Department of Environment, Transport and Regions (DETR) best practice programme on freight distribution and logistics and cross-industry working groups for road, rail and packaging. A Fellow of the Institute of Logistics and Member of the Chartered Institute of Transport, he has written articles and given lectures on logistics. Married with two daughters, one of his hobbies is scuba diving with sharks.

Leigh Sparks is Professor of Retail Studies, Institute for Retail Studies, and Dean of the Faculty of Management at the University of Stirling. He has been employed at Stirling since May 1984. Prior to May 1984, he was employed as a Research Fellow at St David's University College, Lampeter. His first degree is in geography from Cambridge University and his PhD topic was Employment in British Superstores. At Stirling, he is course co-ordinator for an undergraduate course on retail studies and involved in teaching various retail options on postgraduate programmes including the MBA in Retailing by distance learning, and the MSc in Retail Management. He has written widely on his retail research interests. He has undertaken many research projects, including several commissioned by the retail industry and government. He is the co-editor of the *International Review of Retail, Distribution and Consumer Research*.

Phil Whiteoak is the UK Regional Director of Logistics for a large multinational food manufacturing business. He has over 25 years' experience in the FMCG sector and has spent the last 10 years working in the logistics area. He has been extensively involved in the ECR Europe initiative and was co-chairman of the Efficient Replenishment Project during 1995–96.

Jane Winters is currently working as a consultant with Logica UK within the Manufacturing Distribution and Transport Division, specializing in Retail Supply Chain and Efficient Consumer Response. Previously she was a Senior Supply Chain Project Manager with Somerfield Stores, with responsibility for all ECR development projects including Co-Management Inventory, EDI development, cross-docking, short cycle ordering and returnable packaging trials. She initially joined Somerfield in 1994 to manage the non-grocery partnerships with 10 major suppliers including Procter & Gamble, Lever Brothers, Kimberly Clark, Bass Brewers and Pedigree Pet Foods. She has spent the previous 12 years with B&Q, initially managing the Purchase Ledger department and a number of financial systems projects and then took a role in the Logistics area with responsibility for EDI community and message development and for inventory data maintenance on both store and central warehouse systems.

PREFACE

In 1990, John Fernie edited *Retail Distribution Management* for Kogan Page and through academic and practitioner research, case studies and viewpoints, provided readers with a review of retail logistics in Britain at the time. The 1980s had been revolutionary in the history of logistical support to retail stores. Indeed, in this current 1998 edited volume Lawrence Christensen states that the 1980s witnessed the first step change in managing the logistics function. Retailers moved from direct store deliveries (DSD) to centralization of stock at regional distribution centres (RDCs); decisions had to be made about whether all, parts or none of the logistics network were to be contracted out to third party service providers or retained 'in house'; technologies were developed to facilitate logistical efficiencies in the distribution network. Those technologies were either of a materials handling (composite distribution, unitization) or of an IT nature (improving flows of information through the supply chain). These key structural changes in the nature of retail distribution management were reached and documented in the 1990 book. Indeed, it was claimed by one grocery retailer that efficiencies in distribution management accounted for 1.5 to 2 per cent of the healthy net margins experienced by that retailer throughout the 1980s.

The 1990s as anticipated have experienced further change, but instead of structural change which yielded 'one off' large efficiency gains as in the 1980s, this decade has been mainly concerned with incremental improvements and relationship change. Christensen argues that a further step change is needed by all logistics managers if additional costs are to be squeezed out of the supply chain. In the 1980s most retail companies were primarily concerned with physical distribution management and the management of stock from RDCs to stores. Now, retailers are focusing upon the whole supply chain, seeking to also reduce inefficiencies in primary distribution through closer collaboration with suppliers and logistics service providers, and to manage logistics supply better to the final customer. The academic and trade press have been quick to embrace the new jargon of the 1990s – quick response, efficient consumer response, category management, continuous replenishment, and so on. In essence, relationships are the key; the whole supply chain has to be visible in that an efficiency gain in one part of the chain is not negated by imposing additional costs on other parts of the chain. Retailers are in competition as retailers but also as supply chain relationships and partnerships.

This edited volume, *Logistics and Retail Management*, also brings together academics and practitioners to share their research, ideas and experience of retail logistics in the 1990s. The opening five chapters have been written by authors currently based at academic institutions, with the remaining five chapters drawing upon the management experience of industry specialists who have been in the vanguard of logistics change in the 1990s. The aim is to provide a series of research syntheses, reports and results combined with practitioner examples, leading practice and reflections to identify the state of the art/science and the key issues in retail logistics management in the late 1990s.

The early chapters establish the background to the transformation of retail logistics in Britain in the 1990s. Leigh Sparks highlights this transformation in Chapter 1 by charting the development of logistics and the strengthening role of retailers in the logistics channel. He emphasizes the role of relationships in the 1990s and briefly discusses some of the challenges for the future. The issue of relationships is further discussed by John Fernie in Chapter 2 where a more detailed consideration of evolving relationships in the supply chain is undertaken. A comprehensive review of the fundamental tenets of ECR is provided, outlining 14 potential improvement areas where efficiencies can be achieved. Clearly, ECR initiatives have promoted a changing attitude towards supplier–retailer relationships and they have led to cultural and organizational changes within partnering organizations. The latter part of the chapter is devoted to a missing piece of the ECR puzzle, namely, the role of logistics service providers in supply chain relationships. Here, the evidence of a greater commitment to partnerships is less evident than in the supplier–retailer relationship.

The internationalization of retailing has been a developing feature of retailing in the United Kingdom and ignored by British retailers in recent years. Unlike many of our European counterparts, British retailers (with the exception of niche specialist clothing firms) have been slow to internationalize. However, with growth opportunities at a premium in domestic markets, and emerging realization of profit potential abroad, the two largest British grocery retailers have joined Marks & Spencer (M&S) in seeking international expansion. Fundamental to such positions is the quality of the logistics systems. The third chapter, also by John Fernie, seeks to explore the logistical implications of international growth. At the same time it discusses the internationalization of sourcing by retail companies, especially those in the clothing sector. In Chapter 2 it became apparent that ECR initiatives were being adopted in different ways by companies in difficult geographical markets. Chapter 3 develops this theme further to show how retail logistics has evolved in various market environments and how companies are transferring world-class logistics practices from market to market. Logistics excellence provides fundamental competitive advantage.

The internationalization theme and the value of logistics excellence are further developed by Paul Jackson in the aptly titled chapter, 'Taking Coals to Newcastle'. While most clothing retailers in the UK were importing product from the Pacific Rim countries, Marks and Spencer were transporting food and clothing 10 000 miles to Hong Kong. It was in the early 1980s that M&S began to source product from the Far East and realized the opportunity of market expansion in the region. A subsidiary was launched in Hong Kong and stores were developed with 15 envisaged to be open by the millennium. The success of these stores and the increased volume of products moved from the UK stretched the existing supply chain to the limit. It was taking up to 43 days for stock to arrive in Hong Kong by sea and 27 days by air. Jackson documents the reasons for the delays and the 500 actions identified to redress these lengthy lead times. In addition, M&S introduced vacuum packing of clothing merchandise to ensure that it arrived at stores in cleaner condition whilst reducing the amount of space required in warehouses and aircraft.

The final 'academic' contribution is from Martin Christopher and Helen Peck, who continue with the theme of Fashion Logistics, the title of their chapter. The authors claim that there are three critical lead times that must be managed by organizations that wish to compete successfully in fashion markets: time-to-market, time-to-serve and time-to-react. They show that successful companies are 'lean' in that they can reduce lead times and capture information sooner on customer demand. Examples of 'lean' companies and those which have embraced quick response initiatives are given, including The Limited, Bhs and Zara, the Spanish-based apparel company. These cases demonstrate the increasing reach of supply chains from raw materials to consumer and the need for effective management throughout the chain.

It has often been claimed that British grocery retail logistics is the most efficient in the world. Not surprisingly, therefore, a fair amount of space in this book is devoted to the grocery sector, with Phil Whiteoak and Jane Winters providing chapters on ECR initiatives and David Smith and Lawrence Christensen giving detailed reviews of their own companies' logistics operations. Phil Whiteoak begins his chapter with the heading 'ECR – a fad or the future?' Whiteoak's company is a supplier to the grocery trade and he has been quick to point out the implications for suppliers as retailers move to efficient replenishment techniques. His award-winning paper in the *International Journal of Retail and Distribution Management* in 1993 drew readers' attention to the 'downside' of lead time reductions on manufacturers' inventory levels. His chapter in this volume develops this theme further by reviewing the facts and myths of current thinking on efficient replenishment, the key supply side pillar in ECR initiatives. The main thrust of his approach for the future is that logistics practitioners should view supply chain integration across rather than solely along the chain. He argues that there are real opportunities in rationalizing and managing the transport and consolidation functions on an industry rather than a company basis. He finishes the chapter, however, by asking the fundamental question of whether 'the industry is fit for the challenge'.

Whereas Whiteoak's contribution provides an holistic overview of efficient replenishment programmes, Jane Winters looks at one part of this ECR initiative, that of Co-managed inventory (CMI). This chapter is also an update and development of an award-winning paper which Jane received as best paper in *Logistics Focus* in 1996. The chapter provides a case study of the first significant multi-organized trial of CMI in the United Kingdom and possibly Europe. The trial was carried out over a 12-month period between Somerfield Plc and 12 of its leading suppliers, representing a range of branded FMCGs. Winters documents the phases of the trial, the performance statistics and provides an overview of the lessons learnt from the trial for future planning. Indeed, Somerfield has built upon its experience to further develop a supplier partnership programme to avoid 'second guessing' replenishment requirements. It should be noted, however, that few other UK multiple retailers have gone down the Vendor Managed Inventory (VMI) or CMI route.

Company profiles of two of the most respected grocery logistics operations in the UK are then provided. Tesco Plc, the grocery market leader in the United Kingdom, can attribute much of its success in the late 1980s and 1990s to its excellence in logistics management. This was not always true. As David Smith points out in his chapter, the Tesco distribution system almost came to a halt in the 1970s in the wake of Operation Checkout. He cites Powell in that 'Possibly for the first time in its history, the company recognised that it was as much in the business of distribution as of retailing'. Clearly, Tesco learnt from their experience in the 1970s and the company has been in the forefront of logistical innovation with its implementation of composite distribution and the back-up systems technologies. In recent years, Tesco has focused attention on upstream distribution, minimizing the empty running of vehicles and reducing CO_2 emissions through supplier collection and supplier onward delivery programmes. Smith concludes his chapter by looking at future issues, discussing the impact of home shopping, rail for continental sourcing, IT developments and 'green' distribution. The continued drive for excellence is the key theme of Tesco's logistics operations since its near debacle in the 1970s. This search is accelerating.

Similar themes are discussed by Lawrence Christensen in his chapter 'Responding to the Challenges: The case of Safeway'. Christensen appeared in the 1990 edited text where he discussed the integration of the Presto and Safeway networks in the wake of the Argyll Group's acquisition of Safeway UK in 1987. This chapter is an update of Safeway's operation in the 1990s. Christensen shows how the distribution network has been rationalized with 98 per cent of volume passing through 12 distribution centres. The success of this investment in new warehouses and IT systems is reflected in performance over the last five years when volumes have increased by 40 per cent and costs as a percentage of sales have fallen by 0.7 per cent. Christensen warns, however, that costs will only increase in the future unless changes in management philosophy are enacted. Logistics can never stand still. Hence, Supply Chain 2000 is an initiative by Safeway to respond to the challenges of 2000 and beyond.

The final chapter is different. All the previous contributions focused upon ECR, partnerships and how plans were being drawn up to improve the efficiency of getting merchandise through the supply chain. This is only one part (albeit critical) of retailing and retail logistics. In this chapter, John O'Hagan discusses how retailers can improve efficiency in handling non-merchandise stock through the logistics network. He argues that centralization of merchandise stock has become the norm, but when it comes to displays, trolleys, racking, furniture and other non-merchandise items, less attention has been given to the managing of this stock. O'Hagan lists the benefits of adopting a logistics approach to such areas, including centralizing these items, providing examples of M&S, IKEA and Sainsbury which have benefited from Hays' support services in this area.

We decided not to conclude with a chapter on future trends. Would we have been able to anticipate accurately in the 1990 text all the logistics events of the 1990s? We suspect not, other than at a very general level. In any case, many of the contributors in this volume give a view of possible future trends in retail logistics for their own topics. The government's White Paper on Transport has been delayed and is now due to be published sometime this month. Perhaps this delay is due in part to the conflicting evidence submitted to the government's consultation on 'Developing an Integrated Transport Policy'. What we do know is that the government wishes to reduce existing inefficiencies in the transport system, reduce vehicle emissions and improve energy efficiency. These are all sound logistics aims. Many of the points raised by Phil Whiteoak in the latter part of his chapter address these issues. As Whiteoak is co-chair of the UK ECR Transport Optimisation Group, many of the ideas floated here will be piloted in the next year or so. The government predicts that van transport will increase by 10 per cent in the next 10 years. This may be attributed to an increased emphasis on 'City Logistics' whereby larger vehicles are excluded from parts of cities and/or an increase in van deliveries to accommodate the rise in home shopping. This is not 'conventional' mail order home shopping but ordering by fax, telephone, the Internet or tele-shopping from home. At the moment it is difficult to predict the size of this emerging market. Although most picking for home delivery currently takes place at the store, many retailers are investigating specialist picking warehouses for home delivery orders if and when volumes increase sufficiently to warrant such an investment. Those with existing expertise and investment are going to be at the forefront and most likely to be successful. This is but one change in the constantly re-organizing logistics scene. Is this another step-change in the system or a continuation of the 1990s processes of partnership and integration? Who knows if we are at the next stage of retail logistics transformation! Our authors certainly predict exciting and interesting challenges ahead.

John Fernie and Leigh Sparks
Institute for Retail Studies
University of Stirling
Stirling

September 1998

THE RETAIL LOGISTICS TRANSFORMATION

Leigh Sparks

INTRODUCTION

Retailing and distribution are concerned with product availability. This is often summed up in the old adage of getting the right product to the right place at the right time. This implies that retailers must be concerned with the flows of product and information into and through their companies in order to make products available to consumers. In particular, the concern is with the structure and management of logistics channels (Cooper, 1988; Cooper *et al.*, 1991; Bowersox and Cooper,1992; Gattorna and Walters, 1996). The management task is concerned with the elements of the distribution mix (storage facilities, inventory management, transportation, unitization and packaging, communications), which have to be integrated for successful retail distribution. This very success in achieving product availability on a consistent basis makes us often forget just how much effort has to go into retail logistics.

The distribution function manages the distribution mix to provide an appropriate balance for the selected market sector and the company between the lowest possible distribution costs and the highest possible customer satisfaction (Sparks, 1992). Distribution is concerned explicitly with costs and customer service and the elements of decision-making that influence these (Christopher, 1992 a, b, c). To a considerable extent, it is the emergent awareness of the investment required to achieve the optimal balance and the potential service gains that are available that have caused the development of a new professionalism in physical distribution (Drucker, 1962; Lekashman and Stolle, 1965; Bowersox, 1969; Sharman, 1984). The recognition that supply chains and distribution channels had many costs which could be reduced substantially has added to the imperative for management and professionalism.

One consequence of this new professionalism and approach is that the term 'physical distribution' has now been replaced by the term 'logistics' or supply chain management. In many cases the terms are used interchangeably (Langley, 1986) although there are differences. Physical distribution is somewhat narrower than logistics, being concerned with finished products rather than the combination of materials management of components and raw materials, as well as finished products, as implied by logistics. The logistics extension to physical distribution is also concerned with strategic management of the supply chain (Christopher, 1992c; Gattorna and Walters, 1996). Retailers have extended their influence back into logistics management and concepts such as integrated distribution, just-in-time distribution, electronic data interchange, quick response and efficient consumer response are becoming increasingly important, reflecting the scope and power of the retailers and the drive to service and integration. 'Logistics' now has a widespread currency channel and strategic management is more common (Christopher, 1986, 1992 a, b; Dawson and Shaw, 1989a). The logistics concept has also been reflected in the changing nomenclature of professional bodies and academic and trade journals! There is certainly a logistics transformation in the sense of the frequency of the use of the term, but what does it mean in reality for retail business?

Langley (1986) explores this changing terminology by examining the evolution of the logistics concept. He subdivides his (American) chronology into past, present and future. In the period

1950–64, he sees the emergence of marketing practices forcing a reconsideration of distribution, or in most cases transport, costs. Drucker (1962), in a seminal work, focused attention on the need for integration of product movement activities and the opportunities for cost reductions in distribution. Since the mid-1960s, this call has been answered by a commitment to distribution and logistics professionalism. The key elements have been co-ordination, control and customer service. The effect has been the raising of the status of the distribution or logistics functions within companies. Langley's third phase (the future), sees a closer integration among the logistics elements and a concentration on service quality. Whilst there can be arguments about the timing and, to a degree, the content of these phases, Langley is suggesting a progression from a transport operation through a distribution function to a logistics orientation. This is clearly a description of what has occurred and what we broadly understand by the logistics transformation of British retailing. The old inefficient, manufacturer- and supplier-led practices have been swept away by the modern, technologically rich, retailer-led and customer-focused ways of ensuring product availability. This is arguably most advanced in grocery retailing (Kahn and McAlister, 1997; Smith and Sparks, 1993).

This transformation, which clearly affects both manufacturers and retailers and those who supply logistics services, has been in the main a retailer-led transformation. As Grant (1987) amongst many others notes (eg Kahn and McAlister, 1997), there has been a fundamental shift in the balance of power in consumer goods distribution channels. He comments:

> *Until the mid 1960s manufacturers ... were the source of almost all product innovations and new-product developments, they controlled physical distribution in wholesalers and retailers, they were responsible for virtually all product advertising, they exerted a powerful influence on retailers' stocking and display of their products, and they controlled retailers' margins by setting retail selling prices.*
>
> *(p 43)*

The situation today is for the most part totally different, as retailers have dominated in structural, conduct and performance aspects. The activities retailers carry out or organize now include many elements previously undertaken by manufacturers, such as physical distribution. Skirmishes over the price and supply of cornflakes (Kelloggs vs Shoprite), perfume (Chanel vs Superdrug), price-fixing in the electrical retailing market through recommended retail prices and Tesco's campaign against 'selective distribution' through the parallel importing and price reduction (loss-leadering?) of branded products from Nike, Adidas, Calvin Klein and Sony demonstrate both the power of retailers and the battle for supply that has been fought over a long period. These are the high profile extensions to a trend of retailer channel conquest. It is interesting to note the support retailers have in these cases from parliamentarians, newspapers and the public and it is hard not to argue that retailer expansion and dominance have appeared to be strongly in the consumer interest. Times have changed, and distribution has changed with time. Retailers are the channel captains and set the pace in logistics. Having extended their channel control and focused on efficiency and effectiveness, retailers are now attempting to engender a more co-operative and collaborative stance in many channels, recognizing that there are still gains to be made on standards and efficiency, but that these are probably only obtained as channel gains rather than firm gains.

The broad changes outlined thus far are relatively well described in the literature and increasingly understood by practitioners and academics (see, for example, the back issues of *The Journal of Business Logistics*, *The International Journal of Physical Distribution and Logistics Management* and *Logistics Focus* among others). The critical role of logistics in retailing is now well established and is obvious, daily, world-wide. A number of authors have provided convincing descriptions of the changes that retailers have undertaken to their distribution and logistics functions. The pioneering work in this respect in Great Britain has been that of McKinnon (1985, 1986, 1989). The edited collection by Fernie (1990) is important as are the company-based descriptions of

Christensen (1990), McClelland (1990), Millar (1983), Dapiran (1992), Quarmby (1989), Bremner (1990), Sparks (1986, 1988, 1994a), Smith and Sparks (1993) and Walters (1988). Specific aspects of these changes have also received attention as for example in Fernie (1989), Harris (1987), McKinnon (1990) and Mercer (1993). Fernie (1997) has provided a broad review of retail change and logistics change as well as pointing out the international variances in practices (Fernie 1995). Cooper *et al.* (1991) have provided a useful service by summarizing what they see as the key changes in distribution in food retailing (see Table 1.1) and this pattern of change and the emphasis on retail control and domination and the drive for efficiency are accepted as the fundamental pattern of recent British retail logistics. The effect on, for example, stockholding has been quite dramatic (as Figure 1.1 shows for Tesco Stores) – see also Sparks (1994c) – but it is clear from Figure 1.1 as well that the gains from now on are going to be harder to achieve in this area.

In a recent contribution, McKinnon (1996) has attempted to provide a review and summary of this transformation in retail logistics. He identifies six trends, all of which are 'closely inter-related and in most cases, mutually reinforcing':

1. Retailers increasing their control over secondary distribution (ie warehouse to shop) by channelling an increasing proportion of their supplies through distribution centres (DCs). In some sectors such as grocery this process is now virtually complete. British retailers exert much tighter control over the supply chain than their counterparts in most other countries. Their logistical operations are heavily dependent on IT, particularly the large integrated stock replenishment systems that control the movement and storage of an enormous number of separate products.
2. Restructuring of retailers' logistical systems to reduce inventory and generally improve their efficiency through (i) the development of 'composite distribution'; (ii) centralization of slower moving stock; and, in the case of mixed retail businesses, (iii) the establishment of 'common stock rooms'.

Table 1.1 Major logistics innovations by multiple retailers

Period	Problem	Innovation	Consequences
1960s and 1970s	Disorderly delivery by suppliers to supermarkets; queues of vehicles led to both inefficiency and disruption.	Introduction of Regional Distribution Centres (RDCs) to channel goods from suppliers to supermarkets operated by retailers	(1) Strict timing of supplier delivery to RDC imposed by retailer. (2) Retailer builds and operates RDC (3) Retailer operates own delivery fleet between RDC and supermarkets within its catchment area.
Early 1980s	Retailers becoming too committed to operating logistics services in support of retail activity.	Operations of retailer-owned RDCs and vehicle fleets to specialist freight companies.	(1) Retailer can concentrate on 'core business' of retailing (2) Retailer achieves better financial return from capital invested in supermarkets than in RDCs and vehicles.
Mid 1980s	Available floorspace at retail outlets being under-used; too much floorspace used for storage.	Conversion of storage floorspace at supermarkets to sales floorspace.	(1) Better sales revenue potential at retail outlets. (2) RDCs absorb products formerly kept in store at supermarkets. (3) Just-in-Time (JIT) delivery used from RDC to replenish supermarket shelves.

Source : Cooper *et al.* (1991) pp 109–10

3. Adoption of 'Quick Response' (QR), again with the aim of cutting inventory levels. This involves reducing order lead-times and moving to a more frequent delivery of smaller consignments both internally (between DC and shop) and on external links with suppliers. This has greatly increased the rate of stockturn and increased the proportion of supplies being 'cross-docked', rather than stored, at DCs. QR has been made possible

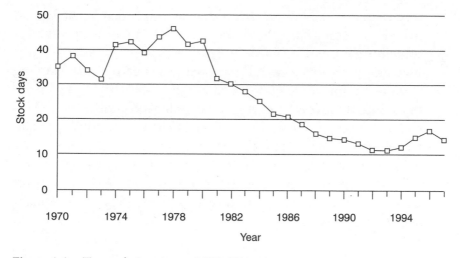

Figure 1.1 Tesco plc inventory 1970–97.

by the development of EDI (Electronic Data Interchange) and EPOS (Electronic Point Of Sale), the latter driving the 'Sales Based Ordering' (SBO) systems that most of the larger retailers have now installed. Major British retailers have been faster to adopt these technologies than their counterparts in other European countries, though they still have to diffuse to many medium-sized and small retail businesses.

4. Rationalization of primary distribution (ie factory to warehouse). Partly as a result of QR pressures and partly as a result of intensifying competition, retailers have been extending their control upstream of the DC. In an effort to improve the utilization of their logistical assets, many are now trying to integrate their secondary and primary distribution operations and run them as a single 'network system'.

5. Introduction of Supply Chain Management (SCM) and Efficient Consumer Response (ECR). Having improved the efficiency of their logistical operations, many retailers are closely collaborating with suppliers to maximize the efficiency of the retail supply chain as a whole. SCM and ECR provide a management framework within which retailers and suppliers can more effectively co-ordinate their activities. As the underpinning

7

technologies for ECR are already well established in the United Kingdom, conditions are ripe for the application of this principle.

6. Increasing return flow of packaging material and handling equipment for recycling/re-use. Retailers are becoming much more heavily involved in this 'reverse logistics' operation. This trend will be reinforced by the introduction of the EU packaging directive. Although the United Kingdom currently lags behind other European countries, particularly Germany, in this field, there remain valuable opportunities to develop new forms of re-usable container and new reverse logistics systems to manage their circulation.

What emerges from these descriptions is something of a generally understood and described set of changes, but a much less understood explanation for these. The extensive concentration process in much of British retailing from the 1980s has possibly produced a more common distribution set-up amongst retailers. General tendencies are well known (see above). What is needed now is a framework within which to discuss these and to place the research that is being undertaken.

UNDERSTANDING THE RETAIL LOGISTICS TRANSFORMATION

The supply chain in much of modern retailing has probably been simplified by the changes described earlier. The channel now consists basically of three main 'actors' – consumers, retailers and manufacturers (it is recognized that there are other important players in the system eg logistic service providers, waste management companies etc, but these three groups are seen here as fundamental in driving change). The previous activities of, for example, wholesalers have been internalized by retailers in the main (McKinnon, 1986). This simplification of the channel structure has, however, been accompanied by a complication of many of the activities within the channel and the demands of, and pressures on, the various organizations have increased. At the same time the 'actors' and organizations themselves have been undergoing change. The links between the channel members take a variety of forms. In particular, the links involve flows of various kinds:

- flows of products (physical supply);
- flows of risk;
- flows of finance (capital and payment);
- flows of information (mandatory and elective).

The concern for distribution has, in the past, been mainly with the first of these, but as a logistics orientation has developed, so too there is greater concern with the integration with these other flows. In particular, the flow of information has been transformed by such an approach, and the flow of finance is increasingly part of the trading terms (Shipley and Davies, 1991), to be used as necessary as, for example, by Burton in extending its payment times (Crewe and Davenport, 1992). Flows of risk are also important and require increasingly to be managed on a global basis (Rovizzi and Thompson, 1992). This combination of flows is well exemplified by Benetton (Belussi, 1987, 1989; Rovizzi and Thompson 1992). Belussi (1989) describes the changes:

> *Benetton's system became more and more flexible: ready to capture minor changes of demand identified by shops, and ready to distribute new orders within the network of subcontracting. IT was the enabling tool . . . shaping every production and distribution stage . . . [it] can be described as an integrated just-in-time system . . . . The main effect of IT was not a simple reduction in the cost of existing functions. It has made possible the development of new functions linking information channels for communication, processing and storing information.*
>
> *(p 127)*

Belussi continues that one of these new functions is 'co-ordination related to financial activity. The franchising system is linked with external venture capital and with Benetton's financial lending system and financial accounts' (p 127). As integral to the company as design and production are, the co-ordination function with its integration of various flows is at the heart of Benetton's operations. The flows with which the company are concerned are much wider therefore than the 'simple' distribution flow. The 'simple' part has been replaced (Kay, 1991).

The idea of risk being integral to the concerns of retailers and the need for the supply chain members to be concerned with more than product flows has also been identified by Crewe and Davenport (1992). In their discussion of changing relationships in the clothing industry they suggest that there is a hierarchy of relationships among suppliers with which retailers are not primarily concerned. Within these relationships, however, they indicate that 'the risk and responsibility again falls on the dependent partner' (p 193). Management of risk is increasingly integral to relationships. At the same time, the dependent partner has changed from being the retailer to the manufacturer (Wickenden, 1992). Senker (1988, 1989) in a number of detailed case studies has pointed to the increasing retailer involvement in product developments and comments that: 'In these instances retailers were largely responsible for the introduction and diffusion of new process plant for processing . . . *and for new distribution methods*' (Senker, 1989: l42, emphasis added).

The power of retailer brands in the United Kingdom and the way in which major retailers (in food and non-food) have developed and utilized this power in association with selected manufacturers reinforce this point. Retailers through their branding have become integral to manufacturing development and to the physical supply of these products. They have altered the distribution system to deal with the rise of retail branding and produced an efficient operation. Further changes linking retailer branding, digital artwork and reproduction (DAR) techniques and packaging have also transformed how packaging is designed and implemented and fits into the distribution channel (Sparks, 1994a).

Figure 1.2 attempts to provide a structure for looking at some of these changes and how they are inter-related. It is an obviously simplistic view, but attempts to suggest that there is a basic set of relationships that are central to an understanding of a retail logistics transformation. While it is true that Figure 1.2 is a major simplification, the complications of reality that can be added to it merely multiply the links and expand the flows. The basic processes remain the same (see ANA, 1992). For example, Crewe and Davenport (1992) point to a series of relationships between preferred suppliers and sub-contracted secondary and other suppliers. While omitted from Figure 1.2, such a complication is diagrammatically simply a case of adding layers to the diagram. It is important to note that the relationships will be linked by the flows noted in Figure 1.2 as it stands. There is thus both added complication and simplification in the channel structure.

Figure 1.2 also contains within it the idea that each of the elements has been changing and that change occurs both within and between these elements. These changes within each element are not the subject of this study, but some comment is appropriate (see Sparks, 1993 and Fernie, 1997). The changes at consumer level have been well identified before and the over-riding change is that of a broadening, deepening and fragmentation of demand. The retailing changes are also relatively well documented. For the purposes of this discussion, distribution changes have not been included here, but rather are included as a component of the 'flows'. Manufacturing changes are also relatively well covered in the literature. The basic concern is the combination or interaction between these elements.

Figure 1.2 attempts to show that the basic groupings are interconnected by various flows as identified earlier. These flows have in the past been transactional in nature, but as the channels have changed so there has been an opportunity to move from transactional based relationships to associative relationships (Dawson and Shaw, 1989a, 1989b, 1990). Much of the research work in buyer–seller relationships has pointed to this change (eg Hogarth-Scott and Parkinson, 1993; Bowlby and Foord,1995; Ogbonna and Wilkinson, 1996). Progress has not always been easy or constant, but the basic position has moved from the transactional to the

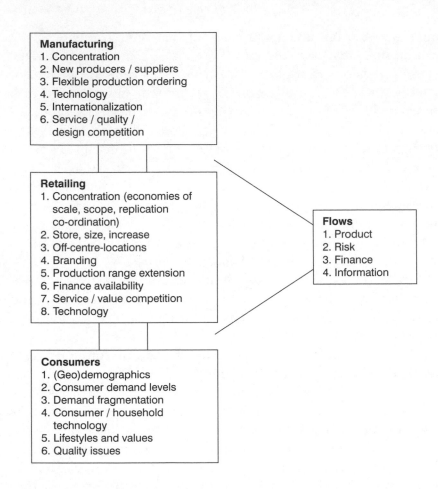

Manufacturing
1. Concentration
2. New producers / suppliers
3. Flexible production ordering
4. Technology
5. Internationalization
6. Service / quality /
   design competition

Retailing
1. Concentration (economies of
   scale, scope, replication
   co-ordination)
2. Store, size, increase
3. Off-centre-locations
4. Branding
5. Production range extension
6. Finance availability
7. Service / value competition
8. Technology

Flows
1. Product
2. Risk
3. Finance
4. Information

Consumers
1. (Geo)demographics
2. Consumer demand levels
3. Demand fragmentation
4. Consumer / household
   technology
5. Lifestyles and values
6. Quality issues

Figure 1.2   Relationships in retail logistics

associative with an emerging focus on integration. It needs to be emphasized, however, that not all relationships are of this form and that while the tendency is identified by research, there are also major sectors where this is not the case in many relationships (eg Crewe and Davenport, 1992; Bowlby, Foord and Tillsley, 1992; Hogarth-Scott and Parkinson, 1993).

In addition to changing themselves, the components of Figure 1.2 do not exist in isolation, and are subject to influences on their performance. In the past, the success of channel operations has been judged mainly by product availability, which is a logistics surrogate for customer service, albeit a simple one. With the emerging capabilities of computing and data capture, so an emphasis on cost issues becomes important. Much of the emphasis in the literature has therefore been on cost and service balances (Christopher, 1986). Increasingly, however, service has been redefined and the new technology has been harnessed to reducing time in the supply chain or cycle (Stalk and Howt, 1990). Time-based competition has become more important (Christopher, 1997). Responsiveness to customer demand has become the key factor rather than product availability. Much of Laura Ashley's problems, for example, can be attributed to poor responsiveness in the logistics chain, as product was held in a form and at points where it could not be responsive to changes in demand. Such lack of responsiveness is now simply too expensive and damaging to contemplate. Characterized in this way, the move from transaction to associative relationships and their integration becomes clearer, as do the frequent exhortations to quick response and just-in-time systems and, more recently, efficient consumer response.

Quick response, just-in-time systems and efficient consumer response are well described in the literature (see reviews in Christopher, 1992 a, b, c; Cooper, 1988; Cooper *et al.*, 1991; back issues of the *Journal of Business Logistics*; Larson and Lusch, 1990; Whiteoak, 1993; Fernie in this volume). In essence, such systems seek to allow quick response to changing demand by holding semi-finished product and using information links to eliminate time in the system. Of necessity such approaches involve the integration of manufacturing and distribution in order to gain the time savings. There is also a growing awareness that as time has a cost, it is important both to eliminate time where possible, but also to move time to its lowest possible cost location. In contrast to Laura Ashley above, The Limited Inc revolutionized the fashion logistics supply chain through their approach to 'elimination rather than engineering' and 'minimum task processing' by which overlap and duplication in processing were eliminated, time in processing was cut and distribution systems were re-thought to eliminate components eg put-away in a warehouse. As an illustration of least cost time usage, products were labelled, pre-sorted etc at production to avoid such activities at warehouse or retail level. This allowed a cross-docking *distribution centre* operation rather than the traditional input, put-away, pick, output *warehouse* operation. The recent emphasis on ECR takes this further by attempting to ensure that suppliers are working with retailers and sharing data so as to avoid unnecessary costs and time delays and to deliver continuous delivery. Somerfield, for example, (see Winters, this volume) held a trial in 1995–96 with 12 suppliers in a co-managed inventory service. The trial focused on the continuous replenishment of products, the introduction of new goods and the management of promotions. It set a 98.5 per cent service level target focusing on the consumer rather than Somerfield. By the end of the trial, stock levels had fallen by 25 per cent without compromising customer service, service levels had increased, and many of the participants had adopted the co-managed inventory technique. Other retailers in similar and different ways are making similar gains (see http://www.ecr-europe.com)

As the pressure for such relationships has increased, so the types of links and/or flows have changed. These changes have focused on four areas:

1. Technology: the role of technology throughout the supply channel and for business re-design (Scott Morton, 1991) should not be underplayed. There is technology introduction at all levels, but the big change has been the integrative nature of a great deal of recent technology investment (Emmelhainz, 1992). This has enabled both the development of an integrative/associative relationship and also the broadening of the logistics concept to include the other flows. In addition to physical product, the other flows, particularly of information, but also of finance and, to an extent, risk, can be integrated into the network. Technology introduction at the retail outlet has been taking place for many years. Retailers have the capabilities of capturing much more data about customers and demand than before. In

itself this is important, but it is the use of these data throughout the organization that is crucial and it is here that the recent investments have made telling differences. Integration within and between companies is now essential and increasingly the replacement of product flows by information flows enabled by such investment is being enhanced by finance and risk flows. Financial flows are increasingly electronic and the technology is also being used to control the risk. An example of the opportunities such developments can bring is Benetton (Belussi, 1987), but an extended version of such systems in a different context is seen in Seven-Eleven Japan Co Ltd where the technology has been used to restructure understanding of consumers, capture demand, place orders, distribute products to stores several times daily, enhance the retail offer by service provision, electronically pay bills and re-structure risk (Sparks, 1994b). The integrative and associative nature of the technology when used in this way is undeniable. The Seven-Eleven Japan example has been extended further by their development and transformation of the Southland Corporation in the United States. Their takeover of Southland has been followed by a radical transformation of the business. Some of this is retail store-based, but much of the effort has been on the distribution system and information collection and transmission operations (Sparks, 1995; Kotabe, 1995; Kunitomo, 1997).

2. Internationalization: the ability of consumers, retailers and manufacturers etc to operate on a much wider scale than previously has also transformed the operations, expectations, outlook and relationships. Consumers have global experiences and expectations in many cases, as well as an increasing ability to purchase globally (through electronic means in many cases). Manufacturers can produce or assemble on a global scale and bring the product or its components to different market places. Retailers similarly are increasingly operating on an international scale whether in terms of sourcing of products or operating of stores. In essence, the flows among the groupings are complicated by their international dimensions and therefore require

closer management. Legal and associative changes such as the EC, NAFTA, ASEAN and other international trading co-operations help such processes. This internationalization or globalization is fundamentally important to modern logistics in that it complicates the situation and adds difficulties. However, technology and communications have improved and specialist operators have extended their coverage and service to make internationalization less problematic in a physical supply sense than it was previously. Transportation enhancements aid this process.

3. Alliances: a particular feature of both the internationalization tendency and the drive towards associative relationships has been the emergence of retail alliances. Alliances have been in existence for some time, but have received a major stimulus in the 1980s and 1990s. Different forms of alliances exist and those commonly identified include promotion-led, buying-led, skills matching, marketing-driven and long-term strategic alliances (Dawson and Shaw, 1992; Ellram, 1992; Robinson and Clarke-Hill, 1995). However, there are also logistics alliances in place (Bowersox, 1990). The relationship which existed between Laura Ashley and Federal Express was one example of such developments, and it also points to the rise of specialist distributors who can take on global distribution on behalf of manufacturers or retailers. It is also clear that many of the companies at the forefront of the changes outlined in this chapter have themselves been characterized by alliances in the broadest sense eg the franchise operations of Benetton, and Seven-Eleven Japan.

4. Management: the final change that requires consideration is that of management. This has a number of components. First, the calibre and type of management that are required for the new methods of operating are very different to previous management requirements in terms of the skills required and the roles to be played. Second, however, in logistics terms there is an issue of whether or not the physical activities and information management need to be carried out by the retailer or the

manufacturer at all. As has been noted earlier, subcontracting distribution to specialist distribution contractors has long been an option, and one that has increased in popularity in recent years. Many of the flow issues are therefore undertaken by others, although controlled by the key participants. Technology provides the ability to control by information rather than by 'doing'. There is thus vertical control, not vertical integration (Kay, 1991). This has concentrated consideration on the potential for contracting out various components of the operations. The amount and type of these subcontracts vary by company but in many cases involve subcontracting the broad range of distribution tasks and associated operations. Such contracts whilst occasionally long-term (25+ years) in existence are subject in most cases to 3- or 5-year reviews. The presence of such a relationship does not, however, mean that price and service negotiations are obviated.

CHALLENGES FOR THE FUTURE

The description and evaluation of the retail logistics transformation above demonstrate both the breadth of the changes and the way in which they all are mutually dependent. The aim in all of this has been to create efficient and effective supply chains to better meet the demands of the customers. Much remains to be done in these areas and integration can go further. In looking ahead, however, it may be possible to see three (inter-linked) areas on which retail logisticians will have to focus in addition to current concerns:

1. Standardization: there remains, despite heroic efforts, a considerable need for standardization across many aspects of logistics. Much can be gained from a better understanding of how minute decisions can affect distribution substantially;
2. Congestion: there is a reliance in most logistics at some time for physical transportation of goods. While for some goods this need is reducing, eg music, books and even academic articles

17

could be Internet delivered, for many products transportation is a problem. As congestion increases, so a concern with movement minimization increases. This could possibly lead in the end to a realistic consideration of electronic shopping and home delivery;

3. Packaging and recycling: finally, growing environmental concern is already forcing retailers to develop better and more efficient recycling and re-use systems. This has a long way still to go, however, and the development of reverse logistics systems is still in its infancy.

REFERENCES

ANA (1992) *Supply Chain Management*, ANA, London

Belussi, F (1987) *Benetton: IT in Production and Distribution*, SPRU, Sussex

Belussi, F (1989) Benetton: a case study of corporate strategy for innovation in traditional sectors, in *Technology Strategy and the Firm*, ed M Dodgson, ch 7, Longman, Harlow.

Bowersox, D J (1969), Physical distribution, development, current status and potential, *Journal of Marketing*, 33, pp 63–70

Bowersox, DJ (1990) The strategic benefits of logistics alliances, *Harvard Business Review*, July/August, pp 36–45

Bowersox, DJ and Cooper, MB (1992) *Strategic Marketing Channel Management*, McGraw-Hill, New York

Bowlby, S and Foord, J (1995) Relational contracting between UK retailers and manufacturers, *International Review of Retail, Distribution and Consumer Research*, 5, pp 333–60

Bowlby, S, Foord, J and Tillsley, C (1992) Changing consumption patterns: impacts on retailers and their suppliers, *International Review of Retail, Distribution and Consumer Research*, 2(2), pp 133–50.

Bremner, D (1990) B & Q: a supply chain revolution, *Focus on PD & LM*, 9(8), pp 10–12

Christensen, L (1990) The impact of mergers and acquisitions upon retail distribution: the Safeway case, in ed J Fernie, *Retail Distribution Management*, Kogan Page, London

Christopher, M (1986) *The Strategy of Distribution Management*, Heinemann, London

Christopher, M (1992a) *Logistics: The Strategic Issues*, Chapman and Hall, London

Christopher, M (1992b) *Logistics and Supply Chain Management*, Pitman, London

Christopher, M (1992c) *The Customer Service Planner*, Butterworth-Heinemann, Oxford

Christopher, M (1997) *Marketing Logistics*, Butterworth-Heinemann, Oxford

Cooper, J (ed) (1988) *Logistics and Distribution Planning*, Kogan Page, London

Cooper, J, Browne, M and Peters, M (1991) *European Logistics*, Blackwell, Oxford

Crewe, L and Davenport, E (1992) The puppet show: changing buyer–supplier relationships within clothing retailing, *Transactions of the Institute of British Geographers*, 17(2), pp 183–97

Dapiran, P (1992) Benetton: global logistics in action, *International Journal of Physical Distribution and Logistics Management*, 22(6), pp 7–11

Dawson, JA and Shaw, S A (1989a) The move to administered vertical marketing systems by British retailing, *European Journal of Marketing*, 23(7), pp 42–52

Dawson, JA and Shaw, SA (1989b) Horizontal competition in retailing and the structure of manufacturer–retailer relationships, in *Retail and Marketing Channels*, ed L Pellegrini and SK Reddy, pp 49–72, Routledge, London

Dawson, JA and Shaw, SA (1990) The changing character of retailer–supplier relationships, in *Retail Distribution Management*, ed J Fernie, pp 19–39, Kogan Page, London

Drucker, P (1962) The economy's dark continent, *Fortune*, April, pp 265–70

Ellram, LM (1992) Patterns in international alliances, *Journal of Business Logistics*, 13(1), pp 1–25

Emmelhainz, MA (ed) (1992) Electronic data interchange in logistics, *International Journal of Physical Distribution and Logistics Management*, 22(8), pp 1–48

Fernie, J (1989) Contract distribution in multiple retailing, *International Journal of Physical Distribution and Materials Management*, 19(7), pp 1–35

Fernie, J (ed) (1990) *Retail Distribution Management*, Kogan Page, London

Fernie, J (1995) International comparisons of supply chain management in grocery retailing, *Service Industries Journal*, 15(4), pp 134–47

Fernie, J (1997) Retail change and retail logistics in the UK: past trends and future prospects, *Service Industries Journal*, 17(3), 383–96

Fiorito, SS, May, EG and Straughn, K (1995) Quick response in retailing: components and implementation, *International Journal of Retail and Distribution Management*, 23(5), pp 12–21

Gattorna, JL and Walters, DW (1996) *Managing the Supply Chain*, Macmillan, Basingstoke

Grant, RM (1987) Manufacturing–retailer relations: the shifting balance of power, in *Business Strategy and Retailing*, ed G Johnson, ch 4, Wiley, Chichester

Harris, DG (1987) *Central Versus Direct Delivery for Large Retail Food Outlets*, Institute for Retail Studies, University of Stirling, Stirling, Working Paper 8703

Hogarth-Scott, S and Parkinson, ST (1993) Retailer–supplier relationships in the food channel: a supplier perspective, *International Journal of Retail and Distribution Management*, 21(8), pp 11–18

Kahn, BE and McAlister, L (1997) *Grocery Revolution: The New Focus on the Consumer*, Addison-Wesley, Reading, MA

Kay, JA (1991) Managing relationships with customers and suppliers: law, economics and strategy, *Business Strategy Review*, 2(1), pp 17–34

Kotabe, A (1995) The return of 7–11 from Japan – the vanguard program, *Columbia Journal of World Business*, 30(4), pp 70–81

Kunitomo, R (1997) Seven-eleven is revolutionising grocery distribution in Japan, *Long Range Planning*, 30(6), pp 877–89

Langley, JR (1986) The evolution of the logistics concept, *Journal of Business Logistics*, 7(2), pp 1–13

Larson, PD and Lusch, RF (1990) Quick response retail technology: integration and performance measurement, *International Review of Retail, Distribution and Consumer Research*, 1(1), pp 17–36

Lekashman, R and Stolle, JF (1965) The total cost approach to distribution, *Business Horizons*, 8, pp 33–46

McClelland, WG (1990) Economies of scale in British food retailing, in *Competition and Markets*, ed C Moir and JA Dawson, pp 119–40, Macmillan, Basingstoke

McKinnon, AC (1985) The distribution systems of supermarket chains, *Service Industries Journal*, 5(2), pp 226–38

McKinnon, AC (1986) The physical distribution strategies of multiple retailers, *International Journal of Retailing*, 1(2), pp 49–63

McKinnon, AC (1989) *Physical Distribution Systems,* Routledge, London

McKinnon, AC (1990) Electronic data interchange in the retail supply chain, *International Journal of Retail and Distribution Management*, 18(2), pp 39–42

McKinnon, AC (1996) The development of retail logistics in the UK: a position paper. Paper prepared for Technology Foresight and available at http://www.21stcenturyretailing.org.uk/ukretail.htm

Mercer, A (1993) The consequences for manufacturers of changes in retail distribution, *European Journal of Operational Research*, 64, pp 457–61

Millar, JL (1983) Distribution in multiple food retailing, in *The Changing Distribution and Freight Transport System in Scotland,* pp15–19, CURR Discussion Paper 8, University of Glasgow, Glasgow

Ogbonna, E and Wilkinson, B (1996) Inter-organisational power relations in the UK grocery industry: contradictions and developments, *International Review of Retail Distribution and Consumer Research*, 6, pp 395–414

Quarmby, DA (1989) Developments in the retail market and their effect on freight distribution, *Journal of Transport Economics and Policy*, 23(1), pp 75–87

Robinson, T and Clarke-Hill, C (1995) International alliances in European retailing, *International Review of Retail, Distribution and Consumer Research*, 5, pp 167–84

Rovizzi, L and Thompson, D (1992) Fitting company strategy to industry structure: a strategic audit of the rise of Benetton and Stefanel, *Business Strategy Review*, 3(2), pp. 73–99

Scott Morton, MS (1991) *The Corporation of the 1990s*, OUP, Oxford

Senker, J (1988) *A Table for Innovation: British Supermarkets' Influence on Food Manufacturers*, Horton, Bradford

Senker, J (1989) Food retailing, technology and its relation to competitive strategy, in *Technology Strategy and the Firm*, ed M Dodgson, ch 8, Longman, Harlow

Sharman, G (1984) The rediscovery of logistics, *Harvard Business Review*, September/October

Shipley, D and Davies, L (1991) The role and burden-allocation of credit in distribution channels, *Journal of Marketing Channels*, 1(1), pp 3–22

Smith, DLG and Sparks, L (1993) The transformation of physical distribution in retailing: the example of Tesco plc, *International Review of Retail, Distribution and Consumer Research*, 3(1), pp 35–64

Sparks, L (1986) The changing structure of distribution in retail companies, *Transactions of the Institute of British Geographers*, 11(2), pp 147–54

Sparks, L (1988) Technological change and spatial change in UK retail distribution, in *Transport Technology and Spatial Change*, ed RS Tolley, pp 123–48, Institute of British Geographers, North Staffordshire Polytechnic

Sparks, L (1992) Physical distribution management, in *Retailing Management*, ed WS Howe, Ch 7, Macmillan, Basingstoke

Sparks, L (1993) The rise and fall of mass marketing? Food retailing in Great Britain since 1960, in *The Rise and Fall of Mass Marketing*, ed RS Tedlow and G Jones, ch 4, Routledge, London

Sparks, L (1994a) Delivering quality: the role of logistics in the post-war transformation of British food retailing, in *Adding Value: Marketing and Brands in the Food and Drink Industries*, ed G Jones and N Morgan, pp 310–35, Routledge, London

Sparks, L (1994b) Seven-Eleven Japan Co Ltd: from licensee to owner in eighteen years, in *Cases in Retail Management*, ed P McGoldrick, pp 336–51, Longman, Harlow

Sparks, L (1994c) Stock control implications of the transformation of food retail logistics, pp. 864–73 of *Proceedings of the MEG Conference*, University of Ulster, Ulster

Sparks, L (1995) Reciprocal retail internationalisation: the Southland Corporation, Ito-Yokado and 7–11 convenience stores, *Service Industries Journal*, 15(4), pp 57–96

Stalk, G and Howt, TM (1990) *Competing Against Time*, Free Press, New York

Walters, DW (1976) *Futures for Physical Distribution in the Food Industry*, Saxon House, Farnborough

Walters, DW (1988) *Strategic Retailing Management*, Prentice-Hall, Hemel Hempstead

Whiteoak, P (1993) The realities of quick response in the grocery sector: a supplier viewpoint, *International Journal of Retail and Distribution Management*, **21**(8), 3–10

Wickenden, J (1992) Restructuring management towards better customer service: a case study, *International Journal of Physical Distribution and Logistics Management*, **22**(2), 16–21

2

RELATIONSHIPS IN THE SUPPLY CHAIN

John Fernie

INTRODUCTION

The 1990s have been the decade of relationships; companies have realized that if you work close to your customers and meet their expectations, they have little reason to choose alternative sources of supply. It is well known that it is easier to retain existing customers than to win new customers, especially those switching loyalty. Relationship building therefore has been a feature of many companies' strategies in recent years, attracting increasing attention in the marketing and logistics literature.

In the fast-moving consumer goods sector, retailers have fostered links with their customers through loyalty cards, although the degree of loyalty to any particular retailer has been questioned (Dowling and Uncles, 1997). Nevertheless, the information derived from EPOS and card data enables retailers to more accurately forecast demand at store level to trigger orders back through the supply chain to retailers' suppliers and subsequently suppliers' suppliers.

It is the purpose of this chapter to discuss these evolving relationships throughout the supply chain. A background to the literature on manufacturer–retailer relationships will be undertaken prior to a more detailed discussion on the role of quick response and efficient consumer response initiatives in improving supply chain efficiency. The final section looks at relationships in providing logistical services and discusses externalizing the logistics function.

CHANGING BUYER–SELLER RELATIONSHIPS

During the last decade the literature on the nature of buyer–seller relationships has shown a distinct shift from the conventional marketing channel approach stressing conflict within relationships to a more planned, focused approach based on alliances and partnerships. Much of the impetus for such change has its roots in materials management, the 'back end' of the supply chain. With the advent of lean production, total quality management and just-in-time deliveries, organizations have been building closer working relationships with a reduced number of suppliers (Macbeth, 1994; Gadde and Häkansson, 1994). The automobile industry has been the focus of much of the research in this area, often charting the historical evolution of the industry and the nature of relationships over time (Womack, Jones and Roos, 1990; Lamming, 1993).

At the 'front end' of the supply chain, similar trends were discernible in consumer markets. At the turn of the decade, Carlisle and Parker (1989) and Dawson and Shaw (1990) introduced the term 'associative' relationship to replace the conventional or administrative channel terminology used in most marketing texts. Since then, the trade press, conference circuit and academic writings have been replete with views on collaboration and partnerships in the supply chain. The Kurt Salmon report in 1993 on Efficient Consumer Response in the US grocery industry kindled particular interest on the savings which could be achieved through greater collaboration between retailers and suppliers. This led to a European comparative report (GEA Consultia, 1994) and triggered a series of conferences and project groups on ECR in Europe (Coopers & Lybrand, 1996; Fiddis, 1997; Mitchell, 1997; Boitoult, 1997).

As can be seen from the above, research has centred upon sup-plier–customer relationships whether these are manufacturer–retailer links or manufacturer–material supplier links. Despite the rhetoric about partnerships, the empirical research undertaken by various writers tends to exhibit a more pragmatic, traditional approach than often is cited in conference proceedings. Two reports, published by the British Institute of Logistics, which surveyed a range of companies from different sectors, showed that effective collaboration is not being fully exploited far less 'partnerships' (Burnes and New, 1995; UMIST/Kearney, 1994). In an analysis of clothing manufacturers and their relationships with their suppliers, Valsamakis and Groves (1996) identified three types of relationship – the partnership, semi-adver-sarial and adversarial relationship. On some variables, performance levels did not significantly differ between class although partnership relationships across the supply chain did achieve a more reliable delivery performance from suppliers with greater flexibility and responsiveness to customer requirements.

In the retailing sector, much of the published research also paints a more confrontational picture than is often portrayed in trade publications. Hogarth-Scott and Parkinson (1993) in their study concluded that 'this research has found long-term but often adversarial relationships between one major UK food retailer and 11 of its suppliers' (p 17). More recently, Ogbonna and Wilkinson (1996) in a wider survey of food manufacturers and retailers claim that relationships are more complex than general discussions on 'partnerships'. Terms such as 'erode their power' were being cited in discussions on how retailers were using own label manufacturers to attack the largest branded manufacturers.

In clothing retailing, similar trends are evident. The restructur-ing of the supply network has been a feature of manufacturer–retailer relationships with a tendency to reduce the supply base and move to preferred supplier status (Crewe and Davenport, 1992; Crewe and Lowe, 1996). The net result has been a more profes-sional approach with greater collaboration on design and fabric decisions. This has led to a more partnership approach although tough negotiations are still the name of the game. 'Things are not perfect now, but they have come a long way. The buyer has a different form of status, it used to be a rule of fear. Some companies still pay lip-service to partnerships, but most suppliers are not treated like dirt as they were in the Eighties' (*Drapers Record*, October 1997, p. vi). Many retailers have a core base and the addition of new suppliers tends to happen when product innovations are introduced. The risks of the new relationships, however, appear to be largely borne by manufacturers; for example, in the UK hosiery industry, Foord, Bowlby and Tillsley (1996) argue that the 'evidence of the power of retailers is that they have been successful in imposing extra costs on manufacturers without any significant loss to themselves' (p 87).

This fear of gaining the benefits but not incurring the costs is also articulated by Whiteoak (1993) who represents a fast-moving consumer goods manufacturer. What is interesting here is that Whiteoak discusses the partnership process in the context of logistical improvements in the UK grocery supply chain as retailers move to sales-based ordering and efficient consumer response. To ensure that a more equitable 'win-win' situation exists, Kumar (1996) argues that relationships must move from the power game to the trust game. He analysed 400 separate manufacturer-retailer relationships and categorized them into levels of interdependence (see Figure 2.1). The top-right category is the 'win-win' box whereby trust was highest, conflict lowest and interdependence was strong. Companies positioned in the hostage category, and drunk with power category have an unbalanced relationship which, without positive action, will lead to a drift into the apathy quadrant.

Kumar (1996) does concede that there are inherent tensions in any relationship and limits of trust are inevitable where a mutually exclusive relationship is difficult to achieve. For example, large supermarket chains stock key manufacturers' brands from competing suppliers; conversely, suppliers need as wide a distribution of their products as possible. Nevertheless, the powerful supermarket chains in Britain, and Marks & Spencer, have been able to guarantee exclusivity of supply by plant, if not product, because of the volumes these major grocers can demand.

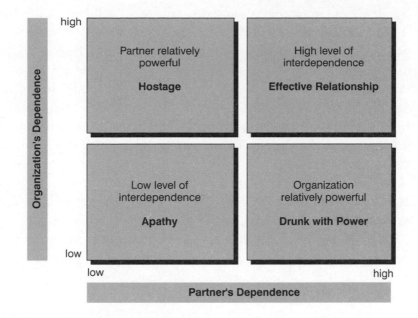

Figure 2.1 Effects of interdependence

QUICK RESPONSE (QR) AND EFFICIENT CONSUMER RESPONSE (ECR)

The origins of both these concepts can be traced back to the United States and work carried out by Kurt Salmon Associates for initially the apparel sector and latterly the grocery sector. Quick response (QR) tends to be associated with the textile and apparel business and has its roots in the response by US companies to increasing competition from Far East and other international competitors. When Kurt Salmon reported that the inefficient, lengthy apparel supply chain was costing $25 billion a year, 20 per cent of the industry's total turnover, the US industry began to instigate a series of initiatives to reduce lead times from primary manufacturer to retail outlet (Christopher, 1997; see Christopher and Peck, this volume). Quick response systems have been implemented by retail firms throughout the 1990s although the concept has still to be embraced by many retailers, especially the smaller firms (Fiorito *et al.*, 1998; Fiorito *et al.*, 1995).

Efficient consumer response (ECR) emerged in the United States partly through the joint initiatives between Wal-Mart and Procter and Gamble and the increased competition in the traditional grocery industry in the early 1990s due to recession and competition from new retail formats. Once again, Kurt Salmon was commissioned to analyse the supply chain of a US industrial sector. Similar trends to their earlier work in the apparel sector were evident; excessive inventories, long unco-ordinated supply chains and an estimated potential saving of $30 billion, 10.8 per cent of sales turnover (see Table 2.1).

ECR programmes commenced in Europe in 1993, a European Executive Board was created in 1994 and a series of projects and pilot studies were commissioned, for example, the Coopers & Lybrand survey of the grocery value chain estimated potential savings of 5.7 per cent of sales turnover (Coopers & Lybrand, 1996).

The European ECR initiative defines ECR as 'a global movement in the grocery industry focusing on the total supply chain – suppliers, manufacturers, wholesalers and retailers, working closer together to fulfil the changing demands of the grocery consumer better, faster and at less cost' (Fiddis, 1997: 40).

Despite the apparent emphasis on the consumer, much of the early studies focused mainly on the supply side of ECR. Initially reports sought efficiencies in replenishment and the standardization of material handling equipment to eliminate unnecessary handling through the supply chain. The Coopers & Lybrand report in 1996 and subsequent re-prioritizing towards demand management, especially category management (see McGrath, 1997), has led to a more holistic view of the total supply chain being taken. Indeed, the greater cost savings attributed to the Coopers study compared with that of Coca-Cola can be attributed to a more narrow perspective of the value chain in the Coca-Cola survey (see Table 2.1).

The main focus areas addressed under ECR are category management, product replenishment and enabling technologies. As can be seen from Figure 2.2, these are broken down into 14 further

Table 2.1 Comparison of scope and savings from supply chain studies

Supply Chain Study	Scope of Study	Estimated Savings
Kurt Salmon Associates (1993)	US dry grocery sector	1. 10.8% of sales turnover (2.3% financial, 8.5% cost)
		2. Total supply chain $30bn, warehouse supplier dry sector $10bn
		3. Supply chain cut by 41% from 104 days to 61 days
Coca-Cola Supply Chain Collaboration (1994).	1. 127 European companies 2. Focused on cost reduction from end of manufacturers' line	1. 2.3% – 3.4% percentage points of sales turnover (60% to retailers, 40% to manufacturer)
	3. Small proportion of category management	
ECR Europe (1996 on-going)	1. 15 value chain analysis studies (10 European manufacturers, 5 retailers)	1. 5.7% percentage points of sales turnover (4.8% operating costs, 0.9% inventory cost)
	2. 15 product categories	2. Total supply chain saving of $21bn
	3. 7 distribution channels	3. UK savings £2bn

Source: Fiddis (1997)

areas where improvements can be made to enhance efficiency. The initial scepticism by some British retailers to this US-imported concept was largely due to the realization that they were already implementing many programmes in those identified areas. As Graham Booth of Tesco comments:

> *ECR is not about space age technology. It is about getting people to use existing tools differently. All of the tools that we've created have been around the industry for years but have not been sweated to the maximum. There's a lot more that we can get out of them just using what we have today.*
> *(Booth in Mitchell, 1997: 58)*

What Booth is alluding to here is that the techniques for supply chain improvement are available but there has been a lack of

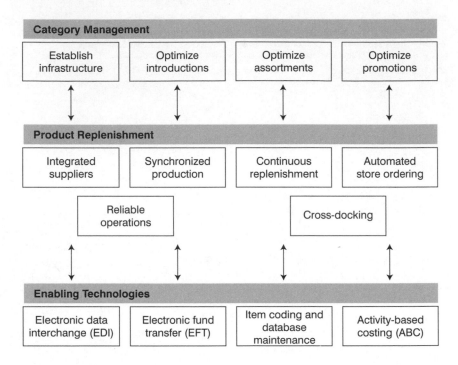

Figure 2.2 ECR improvement concepts

integration across the supply chain, and each of the 14 areas identified for improvements has been probably treated as an individual
sector for management action.

ENABLING TECHNOLOGIES

It is the enabling technologies which are the drivers in making ECR
work. The 1990s have witnessed data overload; loyalty cards
schemes, scanning data, data warehousing and data mining that
have facilitated the understanding of the customer and improved
category management initiatives. EDI allows the transmission of
structured data back up through the supply chain, especially forecasting information. Item coding and database management systems
need to be standardized to ensure that information is sent which is

comprehensible to other partners in the supply chain. Peter Jordan of Kraft Jacobs Suchard claims that 'a lot of companies are throwing electronic data at each other and are not fully understanding the meaning of the data' (in Mitchell, 1997: 34). ECR Europe recommends that the item database should contain the following information:

- item numbers – EAN, retail item number, manufacturers' item number;
- item information – item name, description, dimension;
- pricing information – regular list prices, bracket pricing;
- promotion pricing and conditions – promotion cards, promotion type, effective dates, performance requirements;
- logistics information – case quantities, inner pack quantities, pallet configuration details, truck loading information.

Clearly, a great deal of work needs to be done in this area because a breakdown in communications is possible due to changes being made in one part of the system, such as a new item code or a promotion that is not changed in the data management file. Many of the problems in sharing scanning data and the implementation of EDI networks are related to achieving a critical mass of companies involved to generate substantial benefits.

One enabling technology that has also necessitated working together with partners in the supply chain is activity-based costing (ABC), a successor to direct product profitability (DPP). DPP focused primarily on costs associated with products from buying to ultimate sale on the shop floor. ABC allocates costs according to a specific activity, therefore new product introductions or promotional activities can be added to the more restrictive DPP model.

PRODUCT REPLENISHMENT

The Coopers & Lybrand report identified six key improvement concepts in product replenishment as shown in Figure 2.2:

1. Integrated suppliers.
2. Reliable operations.

3. Synchronized production.
4. Cross-docking.
5. Continuous replenishment.
6. Automated store ordering.

Each stage represents a link in the product replenishment process. The integrated suppliers stage is often neglected despite accounting for 30–50 per cent of a product's cost. The basic tenets of purchasing management, of reducing number of suppliers and fostering deeper relationships with those remaining are important to ensure that flexibility to manufacturers' demands can be achieved. Similarly, synchronized products mean that manufacturers using automated store ordering data can continuously replenish regional distribution centres (RDCs) while at the same time becoming more flexible in manufacturing quantities of a more just-in-time nature.

Most of the research on the implementation of improvements in these areas suggests that retailers have had most impact in product replenishment concepts with continuous replenishment offering both retailers and their suppliers the opportunity to manage their inventory in a more efficient manner (Mitchell, 1997; Fiddis, 1997; PE International, 1997). Where the supplier assumes responsibility for the inventory, vendor management inventory (VMI), the retailer delegates the vendor to generate its orders on sales-based information. The pilot scheme operated by Somerfield is the subject of a later chapter in this book.

CATEGORY MANAGEMENT

As ECR initiatives have moved towards demand management, category management has been the subject of a series of reports, especially those by Roland Berger and Partner (1997) and IGD (McGrath, 1997). The category management process as defined by ECR Europe is made up of eight steps as shown in Figure 2.3 (Mitchell, 1997: 88). Beginning with the definition, which appears straightforward but invariably leads to re-defining categories, each step further stresses the strong marketing emphasis of category management. For example, IGD use bread as an example of how to develop sub-category strategies (see Table 2.2).

While establishing a framework for category management, the three improvement concepts pertaining to demand management are efficient assortments, efficient promotions and optimizing new product introductions. These concepts are linked to the enabling technologies and product replenishment concepts. For example, without accurate locally derived catchment area data, stores cannot provide different assortments for different areas. The problem with efficient assortment concepts is that they can be criticized in much the same way as DPP was in the early 1990s. It is tempting to cut stock keeping units (SKUs) on the basic 80/20 rule or variation of this, namely, that much of the profit comes from a relatively small number of lines. Perhaps the difference in approach during the last ten years is that we now have a better knowledge of our consumers

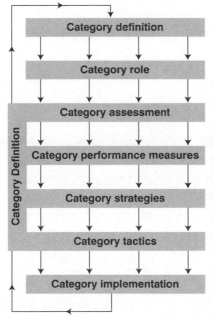

Category definition: to determine the products that make up the category and its segmentation from the consumer's perspective.

Category role: to develop and assign a role for the category based on a cross-category comparison considering consumer, market and retailer information.

Category assessment: to conduct an analysis of the category's subcategories, segments, etc., by reviewing consumer, market, retailer and supplier information.

Category performance measures: to establish the category's performance measures and targets.

Category strategies: to develop the marketing and product supply strategies that realize the category role and performance objectives.

Category tactics: to determine the optimal assortment, pricing, shelf presentation and promotion tactics that ensure the category strategies are implemented.

Plan implementation: to implement the category business plan through a specific schedule and list of responsibilities.

Category review: to measure, monitor and modify the category business plan on a periodic basis.

Figure 2.3 The eight-step process of ECR category management

Table 2.2 Sub-category strategies: the case of bread

Sub-Category Role	Identification Criteria	Strategic Focus	Example
Traffic Building	Attain high market share Frequently purchased, high sales penetration	Draw more consumers into store	Standard white loaf at bargain price
Transaction Builder	Good impulse purchase appeal	Increase average size of transaction	Speciality bread such as Nan or Ciabatta
Cash Generator	High sales and frequently purchased	Generate additional cash flow in category or store	Standard bread products
Profit Generator	High gross margin	Increase category gross margin % and contribution	Added value products such as garlic bread
Excitement Creator	High impulse appeal fits consumer lifestyles	Encourage upgrading to higher margin products	Morning goods such as butter croissants
Image Creator	High quality, premium price/value for money	Create and communicate retailer's image to the consumer	Fresh speciality bread
Turf Defending	Frequently purchased high volume, low price	Defend sales and market share from an aggressive competitor	Own label economy/value type bread

Source: McGrath (1997)

and their buying patterns to know that many slow movers attract valuable customers who spend on other sub-categories.

While product deletion is one problem, the failure rate of new product introduction is increasing. In 1995, 16 000 new items were introduced in the grocery industry in the United Kingdom, an eightfold increase in 20 years. The life expectancy of these products has declined from five years to nine months in this time and 80 per cent of the 16 000 items lasted less than a year (Mitchell, 1997).

Although the ECR Europe Scorecard, a mechanism that rewards progress towards clear goals, stresses the need for integration of ideas, design and research between consumers, retailers and suppliers, the success has been limited. Much time and effort could be saved; however, the dominant influence of retailer private label development in the United Kingdom is often attributed to the lack of progress in this area.

Conversely, optimizing promotional activity is seen to offer some of the greatest potential benefits, for example, the Coopers & Lybrand survey in 1996 estimated that 16 per cent of ECR's total supply cost savings could be achieved by optimizing promotions. This is primarily because promotions are short term, *ad hoc* and in some instances competing with their own brands within a category. Clearly, a better understanding of the drivers behind consumer attitudes to promotions is necessary in addition to identifying and measuring the supply chain costs associated with promotional activity. The additional costs include the individual designing and manufacturing of special packs, item coding and data management changes and the distributing, storing and displaying of promotional material.

MAKING ECR HAPPEN

PE International conduct an annual debate on pertinent logistics issues in the United Kingdom. During the 1990s several years have been devoted to manufacturer–retailer relationships. In 1991 and 1994, the consensus view was that partnerships would not work because of the adversarial nature of existing relationships. By 1997, the ECR momentum had clearly changed attitudes towards relationships. Although reports by PE International (1997) and IGD (Boitoult, 1997) indicate that it is only a limited few companies that are actively participating in ECR projects, there has been a definite sea change in approach to working together to take costs out of the supply chain.

One of the real problems in implementing ECR initiatives is to generalize that all initiatives are good for *all* companies. This is not the case. Each company will have a different starting point and a different agenda. Some companies will already have excellent relationships with their partners, others less so. One thing is certain; partnerships will not take place with all supply chain participants. Retailers have thousands of suppliers and most of them have formed relationships or initiated pilot projects with a very small number of key suppliers (see Somerfield case in this volume). J Sainsbury, a company which has now acknowledged its reactive response to the introduction of ECR in the United Kingdom, has now formed partnerships with its suppliers which have sound logistical expertise (*The Grocer*, 27 November 1997). Furthermore, they have initiated a 'second division' series of initiatives whereby more junior management develop relationships with second-tier suppliers.

What comes across strongly from the trade press and the case studies highlighted by reports is the large amount of management time and resources needed to carry out ECR initiatives. This is why John Rowe, J Sainsbury's logistics director, argues that his company initiated its ECR push through the supply side to allow the demand side to happen. It is clear that category management initiatives are very time-consuming, especially as process change may well lead to cultural change within organizations. McGrath (1997) comments that a project undertaken by a global manufacturer and a retailer had taken six months, equal to 9 000 hours of work, primarily analysing data derived from the initiative.

As relationships develop, the traditional functional boundaries within organizations will change. Coopers & Lybrand (1996: 44) recognized five different types of category management relationship:

1. Traditional salesman.
2. Advanced salesman.
3. Category sales manager.
4. Trusted adviser.
5. Strategic alliance partner.

Their study showed, however, that salesmen categories tended to dominate current sales but the targets set for companies in the future were to plan towards more advanced relationships. It is therefore expected that the traditional organizational structure, the 'bow tie', will begin to break down into multi-functional focus teams (see Figure 2.4). The extent to which companies move down this route will depend on the cultural fit between partners, the size of the respective players and the degree of systems compatibility

(PE International, 1997). Nevertheless, companies have been re-structuring their organizations and McGrath (1997: 45–8) provides examples of UK grocery retailers who have reorganized to take account of category management initiatives.

Although ECR initiatives have clearly promoted greater collaboration between manufacturers and retailers, criticism has been raised about who receives the benefits of the costs saved in achieving supply chain efficiencies. Some concern has been expressed in all the hype over ECR whether the consumer will actually benefit.

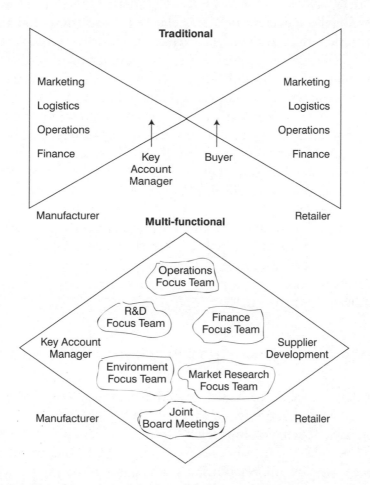

Figure 2.4 Transformation of the interface between manufacturer and retailer

Are these initiatives to enhance margins and improve competitiveness, rather than pass on these savings to consumers with lower prices? Furthermore, is the ECR game one for the big boys, ultimately leading to more concentration of power in the hands of a few, restricting consumer choice and higher prices? ECR Europe and the respective country boards are packed with representatives from the 'major' companies. Not surprisingly, PE International (1997), IGD (Boitoult, 1997) and KPMG (1997) show that smaller manufacturers, especially those with turnovers of less than £5 million, had little awareness of ECR. Retailer participants at PE International's debate in July 1997 claimed that this was a matter of timing rather than attempts at exclusion. Clearly, 'quick wins' on many ECR initiatives require critical mass in terms of resources as well as management commitments. This will tend to favour big over small companies in the short run (O'Sullivan, 1997).

While much of this discussion has focused upon manufacturer–retailer relations, it is important not to neglect relationships further back down the supply chain. If suppliers' suppliers do not go down the partnership route, bottlenecks will occur at the production stage, leading to service delivery failures at RDCs and stores. There have been question marks raised about the centralization of production on a Pan-European scale by major multinationals as this strategy may not enhance flexible response, the basic tenet of ECR. However, Coopers & Lybrand (1996) did highlight how manufacturers and suppliers were moving to a partnership structure away from a traditional adversarial approach (see Figure 2.5).

THE ROLE OF LOGISTICS SERVICE PROVIDERS

Third party logistics providers are 'the missing piece in the ECR puzzle' (Rozemund, quoted in Mitchell, 1997: 60). This quote from the logistics director of Johnson & Johnson International encapsulates the emphasis which has been placed on ECR to date. So much has been written on relationships throughout the supply chain, especially manufacturer–retailer relationships, but the actual

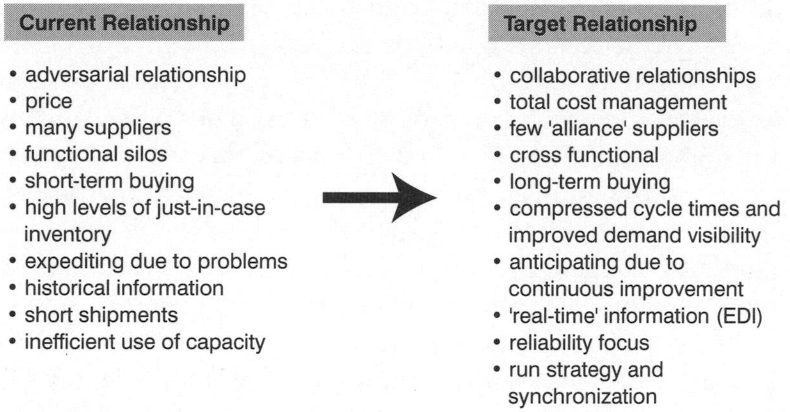

Current Relationship	Target Relationship
• adversarial relationship	• collaborative relationships
• price	• total cost management
• many suppliers	• few 'alliance' suppliers
• functional silos	• cross functional
• short-term buying	• long-term buying
• high levels of just-in-case inventory	• compressed cycle times and improved demand visibility
• expediting due to problems	• anticipating due to continuous improvement
• historical information	• 'real-time' information (EDI)
• short shipments	• reliability focus
• inefficient use of capacity	• run strategy and synchronization

Figure 2.5 Changing relationship between manufacturers and their suppliers

physical process of getting the products to the stores has been largely ignored. Yet the decision on whether to outsource or not is very similar to that of the 'make or buy' decision in operations management. Whether outsourcing occurs or not, a relationship will exist whether it is internal to the organization or to a third party contractor. Although we will focus our attention on logistics outsourcing here, ECR draws a range of third party activities into the equation. As companies move to become virtual organizations and concentrate upon their core competencies, relationships will be formed with outsourcing companies. In ECR, these relationships will be with IT providers, banks, advertising agencies, security companies, in addition to logistics service firms. The theoretical work on outsourcing is based on the seminal work of Williamson (1979, 1990) on transaction cost analysis which has been further developed by Reve (1990) to a contractual theory of the firm and applied by Cox (1996) and Aertsen (1993) to supply chain management. In essence, these authors have revised Williamson's ideas on high asset specificity and 'sunk costs' to the notion of 'core competencies' within the firm. Therefore, a company with core skills in logistics would have high asset specificity and would have internal contracts within the firm. Complementary skills of medium asset specificity would be outsourced on some kind of alliance or partnership and low asset specificity skills would be outsourced on an 'arm's length' contract basis.

Conceptual research tends to establish the context within which the outsourcing decision is taken. Much of this work emphasizes that long-term relationships or alliances are being formed between purchasers and suppliers of logistical services (Bowersox, 1990; Gardner and Cooper, 1994 and McKinnon, 1994). Authors representing the trade have offered advice on what makes a successful partnership or contract and how to avoid pitfalls in these relationships. Good examples can be found in the United States (Tate, 1996; Craig, 1996; Ackerman, 1996) and the United Kingdom (Walters, 1993; Warner, 1994).

Empirical work on the use of logistics service providers and their relationship with purchasing companies has tended to be biased towards surveys of manufacturing companies, especially in the United States (Gentry, 1996; Sink, Langley and Gibson, 1996; McGinnis, Kochunny and Ackerman, 1995; Lieb, 1992; Lieb and Randall, 1996). Indeed, the most recent work on US manufacturing has developed this research into the provision of international logistics services as companies increasingly become global players in terms of sourcing, manufacturing and distributing their products (Daugherty, Stank and Rogers, 1996; Lieb and Kopczak, 1997). UK research has been largely driven by surveys by consultants or contractors, for example CDC (1988) and Applied Distribution (1990), with the periodic surveys of PE International (1990, 1993, 1996) being the most comprehensive. Academic surveys have been limited to Fernie's exploratory work in the buying and marketing of distribution services in the retail market (Fernie, 1989, 1990) and two separate surveys on the role of dedicated distribution centres in the logistics network (Cooper and Johnston, 1990; Milburn and Murray, 1993). Dedicated distribution is very much a British phenomenon in that a single warehouse development is dedicated to one client. Cooper et al. (1992) in their survey of multinational companies based in Europe argued strongly for a 'one stop shop' approach to purchasing logistical services in order to improve efficiency. In practice, this does not necessarily happen. Sink, Langley and Gibson's (1996) survey in the United States showed that buyers were suspicious of the 'one stop shop' approach and 'revealed that buyers are more likely to be seeking the solution for a singular need, or the fulfilment of a specific task' (p 46) and that the 'motivation for outsourcing logistics is routinely related to solving a problem rather than enhancing an opportunity' (p 45).

These empirical surveys have shown that the contract logistics market has grown and the providers of these services have increased in status and professionalism. Logistics is no longer solely associated with trucking but warehousing, inventory control, systems and planning. However, the market is volatile and many of the reasons cited for contracting out such as cost, customer service and management expertise are also used to justify retention of the logistical service 'in house'. There is an impression that companies enter into some form of partnership, but in many cases lip service is being paid to the idea. The PE International surveys have shown over the years that the retail sector, and in particular the grocery sector, has expressed a higher level of dissatisfaction with contractors than in other sectors. In the United States, recent research also shows that greater dissatisfaction is being experienced by users of third party logistics services (Harrington, 1997).

In a survey of British retailers by the author it was shown that outsourcing is still of marginal significance to many British retailers, who have a tendency to retain logistics services 'in house' (Fernie, 1998). Indeed, retail management are much more positive about the factors for continuing to do so than for contracting out such services. Clearly, retailers not only wish to maintain control over the logistics functions but feel that their staff can provide the customer service at a lower cost. As with other industrial sectors, transport is the most likely logistics activity to be contracted out. Despite the growth of the third party market in the 1980s and 1990s, a degree of saturation appears to have been reached in that few companies expected to increase their proportion of contracting out in the future.

The outsourcing decision is a complex one related to the size and historical evolution of the network. Companies with a long history of in-house logistics have 'sunk costs' within the organization, equating to Williamson's (1990) view on asset specificity in the contract relationship. Where these skills and core competencies have high asset specificity, the contract relationship will be intra-organizational, that is, between the retail and logistics departments in a company. Retail businesses with large, complex networks, however, have invariably developed relationships with logistics providers as they have moved into new geographical markets or new retail sectors. This has necessitated the use of complementary skills of medium asset specificity and the development of a range of contractual relationships of an inter-organizational nature (Cox, 1996).

This research showed that the transport function was most commonly outsourced, primarily because the core competencies required are of a residual nature with low asset specificity. Contracts are generally shorter and the relationship is more 'arm's length' in nature or what Cox (1996) classifies as an adversarial leverage type of relationship.

The role of the outsourcing decision has to be seen within the context of a retailer's corporate strategy at discrete moments in a company's history. Acquisitions or demergers, expansion or withdrawal from markets can all influence logistical decisions. No two companies are the same and invariably a third party provider is utilized to solve a particular logistical problem pertaining to a retailer's investment strategy. This 'horses for courses' argument tends to support the work undertaken in the United States by Sink, Langley and Gibson (1996).

CONCLUSIONS

This chapter has illustrated the considerable research that has taken place into relationships throughout the supply chain. The last section has shown that, despite the rhetoric about partnerships, relationships between retailers and their logistics service providers are fluid, perhaps more so than relationships between retailers and their suppliers. Indeed, ECR initiatives have promoted a change culture within partnering organizations. It has been recognized that to achieve greater supply chain efficiencies and cost savings, the 14 improvement areas outlined in Figure 2.2 can only succeed through greater collaboration between members of the supply chain. At present, ECR is in its infancy and research has shown that pilot projects and other initiatives tend to be limited to the larger 'blue chip' organizations. Nevertheless, ECR has promoted an awareness of the issues pertaining to supply chain improvements, which augurs well for collaboration by companies, including small and medium-sized firms, in the future.

REFERENCES

Ackerman, KB (1996) Pitfalls in logistics partnerships, *International Journal of Physical Distribution and Logistics Management*, 26(3), pp 35–7

Aertsen, F (1993) Contracting out the physical distribution function: a trade-off between asset specificity and performance measurement, *International Journal of Physical Distribution and Logistics Management*, 23(1) pp 26–8

Applied Distribution (1990) *Third Party Contract Distribution*, Applied Distribution Ltd., Maidstone

Boitoult, L (1997) *Building the Foundations: An Introduction to Total Supply Chain Management*, Institute of Grocery Distribution, Watford

Bowersox, PJ (1990) The strategic benefits of logistics alliances, *Harvard Business Review*, 68(4), pp 36–45

Burnes, B and New, S (1995) *Strategic Advantage and Supply Chain Collaboration*, Institute of Logistics, Corby.

Carlisle, JA and Parker, RC (1989) *Beyond Negotiation*, Wiley, Chichester

Christopher, M (1997) *Marketing Logistics*, Butterworth-Heinemann, London

Cooper, J, Browne, M and Peters, M (1991) *European Logistics: Markets, Management and Strategy*, Blackwell, Oxford

Cooper, J and Johnston, M (1990) Dedicated contract distribution: an assessment of the UK market place, *International Journal of Physical Distribution and Logistics Management*, 20(1), pp 25–31

Coopers & Lybrand (1996), *European Value Chain Analysis Study – Final Report*, ECR Europe, Utrecht.

Corporate Development Consultants (CDC) (1988) *The UK Market for Contract Distribution*, CDC, London

Cox, A (1996) Relationship competence and strategic procurement management. Towards an entrepreneurial and contractual theory of the firm, *European Journal of Purchasing and Supply Management*, 2(1), pp 57–70

Craig, T (1996) Outsourcing: let the buyers beware, *Transport and Distribution*, 37(5), pp 1–3

Crewe, L and Davenport, E (1992) The puppet show: changing buyer-seller relationships within clothing retailing, *Transactions of the Institute of British Geographers*, 17, pp 183–97

Crewe, L and Lowe, M (1996) United Colours? Globalisation and localisation tendencies in fashion retailing, in *Retailing Consumption and Capital: Towards the New Retail Geography*, ed N Wrigley and M Lowe, ch 15, Longman, Harlow

Daugherty, PJ, Stank, TP and Rogers, DS (1996) Third-party logistics service providers: purchasers' perceptions, *International Journal of Purchasing and Materials Management*, 32(2), pp 7–16

Dawson, JA and Shaw, S (1990) The changing character of retailer-supplier relationships, in *Retail Distribution Management*, ed J Fernie, ch 1, Kogan Page, London

Dowling, GR and Uncles, M (1997) Do customer loyalty programs really work?, *Sloan Management Review*, Summer, pp 71–82

Fernie, J (1989) Contract distribution in multiple retailing, *International Journal of Physical Distribution and Materials Management*, 19(7), pp 1–35

Fernie, J (1990) Third party or own account – trends in retail distribution, in *Retail Distribution Management: A Strategic Guide to Developments and Trends*, ed J Fernie, Kogan Page, London

Fernie, J (1998) Outsourcing distribution in UK retailing, *Research Paper No. 9801*, University of Stirling, Stirling, Scotland

Fiddis, C (1997) *Manufacturer-Retailer Relationships in the Food and Drink Industry: Strategies and Tactics in the Battle for Power*, FT Retail & Consumer Publishing, Pearson Professional, London

Fiorito, SS, Giunipero, LC and Yan, H (1998) Retail buyers' perceptions of quick response systems, *International Journal of Retail and Distribution Management*, 26(6), pp 237–46

Fiorito, SS, May, EG and Straughn, K (1995) Quick response in retailing: components and implementation, *International Journal of Retail and Distribution Management*, 23(5), pp 12–21

Foord, J, Bowlby, S and Tillsley, C (1996) The changing place of retailer-supplier relations in British retailing, in *Retailing Consumption and Capital: Towards the New Retail Geography*, ed N Wrigley and M Lowe, ch 4, Longman, Harlow.

Gadde, L-E and Häkansson, H (1994) The changing role of purchasing: reconsidering three strategic issues, *European Journal of Purchasing and Supply Management*, 1(1), pp 27–35

Gardner, J and Cooper, M (1994) Partnerships: a natural evolution in logistics, *Journal of Business Logistics*, 15(2), pp 121–44

GEA Consultia (1994) *Supplier-Retailer Collaboration in Supply Chain Management*, Coca-Cola Retailing Research Group Europe, London

Gentry, JJ (1996) Carrier involvement in buyer-seller supplier strategic partnerships, *International Journal of Physical Distribution and Logistics Management*, 26(3), pp 14–25

Harrington, LH (1997) Growing up: two surveys suggest that the robust, youthful logistics-outsourcing industry may have reached the brink of maturity, *Industry Week*, **246**(19), pp 136–40

Hogarth-Scott, S and Parkinson, ST (1993) Retailer-supplier relationships in the food channel – a supplier perspective, *International Journal of Retail and Distribution Management*, 21(8), pp 12–19

KPMG (1997) UK food manufacturing: an industry-wide survey, KPMG, London

Kumar, N (1996) The power of trust in manufacturer-retailer relationships, *Harvard Business Review*, **74,** November/December, (6), pp 92–106

Kurt Salmon (1993) *Efficient Consumer Response: Enhancing Consumer Value in the Supply Chain*, Kurt Salmon, Washington, DC

Lamming, R (1993) *Beyond Partnership: Strategies for Innovation and Lean Supply*, Prentice-Hall, Hemel Hempstead

Lieb, R (1992) The use of third party logistics services by large American manufacturers, *Journal of Business Logistics*, 13(2), pp 29–41

Lieb, RC and Kopczak, L (1997) CEO perspectives in the current status and future prospects of US third party logistics service providers, paper presented at the conference of the Institute of Logistics, University of Huddersfield, Huddersfield

Lieb, RC and Randall, M (1996) A comparison of the use of third-party logistics services by large American manufacturers, 1991, 1994 and 1995, *Journal of Business Logistics,* 17(1), pp 305–20

Macbeth, DK (1994) The role of purchasing in a partnering relationship, *European Journal of Purchasing and Supply Management*, 1(1), pp 19–25

McGinnis, MA, Kochunny, CM and Ackerman, KB (1995) Third party logistics choice, *The International Journal of Logistics Management*, 6(2), pp 93–102

McGrath, M (1997) *A Guide to Category Management*, IGD, Letchmore Heath

McKinnon, AC (1994) The purchase of logistical services, in *Logistics and Distribution Planning*, ed J Cooper, ch 17, Kogan Page, London

Milburn, J and Murray, W (1993) Saturation in the market for dedicated contract distribution, *Logistics Focus*, 1(5), pp 6–9

Mitchell, A (1997) *Efficient Consumer Response: A New Paradigm for the European FMCG Sector*, FT Retail & Consumer Publishing, Pearson Professional, London

Ogbonna, E and Wilkinson, B (1996) Inter-organisational power relations in the UK grocery industry: contradictions and developments, *The International Review of Retail, Distribution and Consumer Research*, 6(4), pp 395–414

O'Sullivan, D (1997) ECR – will it end in tears?, *Logistics Focus*, 5(7), pp 2–5

PE International (1990) *Contract Distribution in the UK: What the Customers Really Think*, PE International, Egham

PE International (1993) *Contracting-out or Selling out?*, PE International, Egham

PE International (1996) *The Changing Role of Third Party Logistics: Can the Customer Ever be Satisfied?*, PE International, Egham

PE International (1997), *Efficient Consumer Response: Supply Chain Management for the New Millennium*, Institute of Logistics, Corby

Reve, T (1990) The firm as a means of internal and external contracts, in *The Firm As a Nexus of Treaties,* ed M Aoki *et al.*, pp 136–88, Sage, London

Roland Berger and Partner (1997) *Category Management Best Practice Report*, ECR Europe, Utrecht

Sink, HL, Langley, CJ and Gibson, BJ (1996) Buyer observations of the US third-party logistics market, *International Journal of Physical Distribution and Logistics Management,* **26**(3), pp 38–46

Tate, K (1996) The elements of a successful logistics partnership, *International Journal of Physical Distribution and Logistics Management,* **26**(3), pp 7–13

UMIST/Kearney (1994) *Partnership or Powerplay*, Institute of Logistics, Corby

Valsamakis, V and Groves, OG (1996) Supplier-customer relationships: do partnerships perform better?, *Journal of Fashion Marketing and Management*, **1**(1), pp 9–25

Walters, PJ (1993) *In or Out? The Contract Distribution Dilemma*, Distribution Dynamics, Sevenoaks

Warner, B (1994) *Making the Right Choice: A Guide to Distribution Solutions*, Institute of Logistics, Corby

Whiteoak, P (1993) The realities of quick response in the grocery sector: a supplier viewpoint, *International Journal of Retail and Distribution Management*, **21**(8), pp 3–10

Williamson, OE (1979) Transaction-cost economics: the governance of contractual relations, *Journal of Law and Economics*, **22**, pp 232–61

Williamson, OE (1990) The firm as a nexus of treaties: an introduction, in *The Firm As a Nexus of Treaties*, ed M Aoki *et al.*, Sage, London

Womack, J, Jones, D and Roos, D (1990) *The Machine that Changed the World*, Rawson Associates, New York

3

THE INTERNATIONALIZATION OF THE RETAIL SUPPLY CHAIN

John Fernie

INTRODUCTION

The internationalization of retailing has attracted considerable academic attention in the 1990s. Two edited texts (Akehurst and Alexander, 1996; McGoldrick and Davies, 1995) and two single authored texts (Alexander, 1997; Sternquist, 1998) bear witness to the increasing importance of internationalization within the retail literature. This interest can only increase as national and super-regional companies view global expansion as the major route to growth in the twenty-first century. The theme of the Retail Week Conference in the United Kingdom in 1998 was world-class retailing and in his opening address to delegates Terry Leahy, Chief Executive of Tesco, was quick to point out that UK companies have a lightweight presence in global markets, something which his company hopes to change in the future. Leahy's point can be backed up by figures from *Stores* magazine of January 1998 and Corporate Intelligence on Retailing (1998) which show that Tesco, positioned at number 18, is the first UK retailer in the global list languishing behind US, French and German retailers. Similarly, on the European stage, Tesco at number 12, and J Sainsbury at 14 are the only two in the top 20 in a list dominated by German and French retailers.

Despite all of the hype about international retailing, little has been written about the supply chain implications of the internationalization process. Sparks (1995) acknowledges that there are three main threads to understanding retail internationalization:

1. International sourcing.
2. International retail operations.
3. Internationalization of management ideas.

Of these, most researchers have concentrated upon retail operations, but by that they mean store, not logistics, operations. Nevertheless, with the internationalization of key logistics concepts such as quick response and ECR, it quickly became apparent that countries were at very different stages of the adoption process of these concepts. Distribution 'cultures' vary within and between countries; hence companies seeking to expand into new markets need to be cognisant of the macro-environmental factors that they will face in these markets. This chapter will seek to explore how retail logistics has evolved in different market environments and how companies are transferring world-class logistics practices from market to market. Prior to discussing these issues, however, it is appropriate to comment upon international sourcing.

INTERNATIONAL SOURCING

Although the current debate on global strategies of retailers takes the form of entry to new geographical markets, most retailers are already familiar with the internationalization process through their sourcing policies. In much the same way as manufacturers have sought 'offshore' production to reduce the costs of the manufactured product, retailers have looked beyond their domestic markets to source products of acceptable quality at competitive prices. It has been the apparel sector which has led in international sourcing policies with US and European companies targeting Pacific Rim nations for finished and semi-finished products. The lengthening of the supply chain clearly has given logistics managers of these companies a set of challenges in terms of the cost trade-offs with regard to better buying terms but increased distribution costs. The US company, The Limited, revolutionized the fashion retail market in the United States through its global procurement strategy which is underpinned by state-of-the-art technology from computer-aided design to EDI links with suppliers. Those suppliers in Southeast Asia have their goods consolidated in Hong Kong from where four chartered jumbo jets fly direct to their Columbus, Ohio, distribution centre for onward distribution to their stores. This enabled the company to turn its inventory twice as quickly as the average for a US speciality store.

It is not only the textile markets which have witnessed an increased globalization of sourcing, similar trends are evident in the grocery sector. As consumers acquire more cosmopolitan tastes and grocery retailers have developed their product ranges over the last 10 to 15 years, it is inevitable that many products cannot be sourced from the domestic market. None the less, grocery retailers in the United Kingdom invariably source some products from other parts of the EU outwith the United Kingdom, not because of geographical or climatic reasons but because of the ability of non-UK suppliers to provide products in the volume, quality, variety and price to meet the demands of buyers (see Shaw, Dawson and Blair, 1992 for a discussion on imported foods for the Safeway chain in the UK).

The internationalization of sourcing in the Safeway case has been facilitated by the liberalization of markets in the European Union in the 1990s. This has been replicated in North America with the North American Free Trade Agreement (NAFTA) and the overall policies of the UN's World Trade Organization at liberalizing trade on a global scale. In the EU, for example, a natural consequence of the harmonization of markets in Europe has been for more manufacturing companies to treat the EU as one, rather than a host of individual national markets. Thus the removal of trade barriers, the deregulation of transport, especially road transport, and the acceptance of uniform standards in information systems, have all promoted the re-engineering of manufacturers' supply chains.

Examples of case studies of companies are quoted in conference papers (Machel, 1993; Harland, 1994) and monographs (Cooper, 1993; Davis, 1995; Holmes, 1995). While the trend for most manufacturing companies has been to service European markets from a single or limited number of distribution centres, much depends on the nature of the product supplied. In the EIU's survey of European companies, food companies still favoured the country warehouse model (bucking the trend) and consumer goods suppliers opted for a regional sub-division structure rather than a pan-European solution (Holmes, 1995). Nevertheless, in the survey and others (St Quentin, 1993), The Netherlands, in particular, and the Benelux countries, in general, were the favoured locations for regional distribution centre investment by multinational corporations. It should be noted, however, that Daniel Jones from Cardiff Business School has questioned this rationalization of networks, especially the move to larger manufacturing plants serving wider geographical areas, primarily in that such a strategy may conflict with the basic tenets of an ECR strategy which promotes flexibility and smaller production runs (in Mitchell, 1997).

While accepting that a degree of internationalization is inevitable as trade barriers are removed, the international development of a retailer's store network poses another set of problems pertaining to sourcing decisions. In the same way as Japanese automobile companies have re-configured their supply chain by creating a new network of suppliers in Europe and North America, retailers going global have to decide whether to source from traditional suppliers or seek new suppliers. Much will depend on the nature of the entry strategy. If entry is through organic growth, it may be possible to supply from the existing network; if a joint venture or an acquisition occurs, the retailer has to decide whether to retain or change the supply base which it inherited. If we take the case of J Sainsbury, nearer home it entered the Northern Ireland market with an organic growth strategy reassuring representatives of the Province that it would generate considerable business for Irish suppliers; in the United States, its gradual takeover of the Shaws and Giant chains has led to a radical transformation of its supplier base (Wrigley, 1997a and b).

In a similar way, Tesco's acquisition of ABF in Ireland will lead to a transformation of a distribution culture which is akin to the situation in Britain in the mid-1980s. Hence, it can be argued that foreign competition or even the threat of competition has produced changes in supply chain practices. Indeed, the advent of ECR and quick response can be attributed to traditional players in the US apparel and grocery sectors facing competition from new formats. Most of the success stories pertaining to the internationalization of the retail supply chain tend to relate to companies that have exerted strong control over their supply chain activities. This means the development of strong relationships with suppliers, the implementation of integrated technology systems and the willingness to be flexible in a changing market place. It is also no coincidence that some of these companies (Wal-Mart, Benetton) have narrow product assortments. It should be noted that The Limited, although it is not an international firm in terms of store development, derived its name from its narrow range of high fashion sportswear. This streamlines and simplifies the logistical network. The success of Benetton can be attributed to all of these factors listed above. The company always has been at the forefront of technological efficiency from garment design, production, automated warehouses and the invoicing and transmission of orders by EDI. Its manufacturing operation is flexible and involves a network of 200 suppliers and 850 sub-contractors in close proximity to its main factory in Ponzano Veneto. 'Benetton's long-term investment in logistics efficiency has been repaid with the fastest cycle times in the industry, no excess work in progress, little residual stock to be liquidated at the end of the season, and near perfect customer service' (Christopher, 1997: 127–8)

By contrast, another vertically integrated company with a strong international brand name, Laura Ashley, has shown how a disastrous logistics operation can lead to the near demise of a company. In the early 1990s, the company began to incur losses, primarily because it could not deliver to its stores in time to meet a season's collection. It developed a series of unco-ordinated management information systems which meant that orders invariably were not met despite its five major warehouses having over 55 000 lines of inventory (of which 15 000 were current stock). In addition, relationships with clothing suppliers, freight forwarders and transport companies were piecemeal and transactional in nature (Peck and Christopher, 1994). In 1992 Laura Ashley contracted out its entire logistics operation to Federal Express with a view to upgrading its systems and utilizing Federal Express' global network to minimize stock levels. Although Laura Ashley's logistics performance improved markedly in the following years, it terminated the contract in 1996, less than halfway through the 10-year deal. Laura Ashley's continuing poor financial results in the late 1990s are perhaps a reflection on losing customer confidence in the 1990s. Whilst logistics can give companies competitive advantage, in this case non-availability of product in stores and catalogues lost Laura Ashley goodwill and market share in what was becoming an increasingly competitive clothing market.

DIFFERENCES IN DISTRIBUTION 'CULTURE' IN INTERNATIONAL MARKETS

It was shown in Chapter 2 how ECR principles have been adopted at different stages by different companies in international markets; also, in the previous section it was noted that new entrants to a market can change the distribution culture of that market. Differences in such markets are more likely to exist in the context of fast-moving consumer goods products, especially groceries, because of the greater variations in tastes which occur in not only national but regional markets. The catalyst for much of the interest in these international comparisons was the revealing statistic from the Kurt Salmon report in 1993 that it took 104 days for dry grocery products to pass through the US supply chain from the suppliers' picking line to the checkout. With the advent of ECR, it was hoped to reduce this time to 61 days, a figure which was still behind the lead times encountered in Europe, especially in the United Kingdom where inventory in the supply chain averages around 25 days (see the GEA, 1994, report for further details).

Mitchell (1997: 14) explains the differences between the United States and Europe in terms of trading conditions. He states the following:

- The US grocery retail trade is fragmented, not concentrated as in parts of Europe.
- US private label development is primitive compared with many European countries.
- The balance of power in the manufacturer–retailer relationship is very different in the United States compared to Europe.
- The trade structure is different in that wholesalers play a more important role in the United States.
- Trade practices such as forward buying were more deeply rooted in the United States than in Europe.
- Trade promotional deals and the use of coupons in consumer promotions are unique to the United States.
- Legislation, especially anti-trust legislation, can inhibit supply chain collaboration.

Fernie (1994; 1995) cites the following factors to explain these variations in supply chain networks:

- the extent of retail power;
- the penetration of store brands in the market;
- the degree of supply chain control;
- types of trading format;
- geographical spread of stores;
- relative logistics costs;
- level of IT development;
- relative sophistication of the distribution industry.

Of these eight factors, they can be classified into those of a relationship nature, the first three, and operational factors. Clearly, there has been a significant shift in the balance of power between manufacturer and retailer during the last 20 to 30 years as retailers increasingly take over responsibility for aspects of the value-added chain, namely, product development, branding, packaging and marketing. As merger activity continues in Europe, retailers have grown in economic power to dominate their international branded manufacturer suppliers (see Table 3.1). While there are different levels of retail concentration at the country level, the trend is for increased concentration even in the southern European nations that are experiencing an influx of French, German and Dutch retailers.

By contrast, Ohbora *et al.* (1992) maintain that this power struggle is more evenly poised in the United States where the grocery market is more regional in character, enabling manufacturers to wield their power in the marketplace. This, however, is likely to change as Wal-Mart develops its supercenters and becomes the first national grocery retailer by the turn of the century.

Commensurate with the growth of these powerful retailers has been the development of distributor labels. This is particularly relevant in the United Kingdom, whereby supermarket chains have followed the Marks & Spencer strategy of strong value-added brands that can compete with manufacturers' brands. As can be seen from Figure 3.1, British retailers dominate the list of top 25 own

Table 3.1 Comparison of European sales of top FMCG manufacturers and retailers, 1993–94

Manufacturers Company	Sales (bn ecu)	Retailers Company	Sales (bn ecu)
Unilever	18.44	Metro	43.40
Nestle	17.65	Rewe	24.41
Philip Morris	14.14	Tengelmann	20.94
BSN (Danone)	10.00	Promodes	20.90
Procter and Gamble	6.91	Edeka	20.61
Mars	4.63	Leclerc	19.50
Allied Domecq	4.48	Intermarché	18.85
Guinness	3.14	Aldi	16.60
Grand Metropolitan	4.14	Carrefour	16.32
Heineken	3.06	Sainsbury	12.02
Top 10 total	85.59	Top 10 total	213.55

Note: Mark-up exchange rate used: FT 12/10/95
Source: Fiddis, 1997

label retailers in Europe. In the United States, own label products accounted for 15 per cent of sales in US supermarkets (Fiddis, 1997). This will change, however, with the drive by Wal-Mart to link its supercenter format and own label strategy in addition to the expansion by European retailers such as Ahold and J Sainsbury which have high own label penetration in their domestic markets.

The net result of this shift to retail power and own label development has been that manufacturers have been either abdicating or losing their responsibility for controlling the supply chain. In the United Kingdom the transition from a supplier-driven system to one

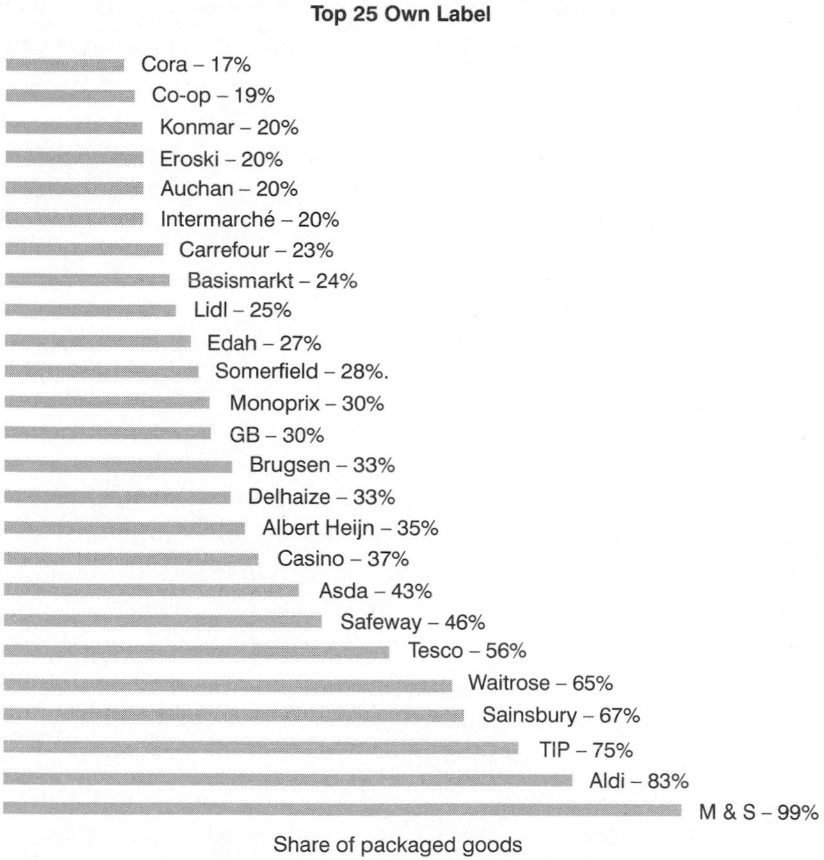

Top 25 Own Label

Cora – 17%
Co-op – 19%
Konmar – 20%
Eroski – 20%
Auchan – 20%
Intermarché – 20%
Carrefour – 23%
Basismarkt – 24%
Lidl – 25%
Edah – 27%
Somerfield – 28%.
Monoprix – 30%
GB – 30%
Brugsen – 33%
Delhaize – 33%
Albert Heijn – 35%
Casino – 37%
Asda – 43%
Safeway – 46%
Tesco – 56%
Waitrose – 65%
Sainsbury – 67%
TIP – 75%
Aldi – 83%
M & S – 99%

Share of packaged goods

Figure 3.1   Own-label penetration by retailer

of retail control is complete compared with some parts of Europe and the United States.

Of the operational factors identified by Fernie (1994), the nature of trading format has been a key driver in shaping the type of logistics support to stores. For example, in the United Kingdom the predominant trading format has been the superstore in both food and specialist household products and appliances. This has led to the development of large regional distribution centres (RDC) for the centralization of stock from suppliers. In the grocery sector, supermarket operations have introduced composite warehousing and trucking whereby products of various temperature ranges can be stored in one warehouse and transported in one vehicle. This has been possible because of the scale of the logistics operation, namely, large RDCs supplying large superstores. In the rest of Europe, by contrast, most of the leading companies are involved in a wide range of formats and markets. For example, Intermarché, listed as number 6 in Table 3.1, has three 101 outlets supplied by 41 RDCs, including an RDC for hard discounters, 17 for dry grocery and 19 for fresh and frozen products.

The size and spread of stores will therefore determine the form of logistical support to retail outlets. Geography also is an important consideration in terms of the physical distances products have to be moved in countries such as the United Kingdom, The Netherlands and Belgium compared with the United States and, to a lesser extent, France and Spain. Centralization of distribution into RDCs was more appropriate to urbanized environments where stores could be replenished regularly. By contrast, in France and Spain some hypermarket operators have few widely dispersed stores, often making it more cost-effective to hold stock in store rather than at an RDC.

The question of a trade-off of costs within the logistics mix is therefore appropriate at a country level. Labour costs permeate most aspects of the logistics mix – transport, warehousing, inventory and administration costs. Not surprisingly, dependence on automation and mechanization increases as labour costs rise (the Scandinavian countries have been in the vanguard of innovation here because of high labour costs). Similarly, it can be argued that UK retailers, especially grocery retailers, have been innovators in ECR principles because of high inventory costs, because of high interest rates in the 1970s and 1980s. This also is true of land and property costs. In Japan, the United States and the Benelux countries the high cost of retail property acts as an incentive to maximize sales space and minimize the carrying of stock in store. In France and the United States the relatively lower land costs lead to the development of rudimentary warehousing to house forward buy and promotional stock.

In order to achieve cost savings throughout the retail supply chain, it will be necessary for collaboration between parties to implement the ECR principles discussed in Chapter 2. The 'enabling technologies' identified by Coopers & Lybrand (1996) are available, but their implementation is patchy both within and between organizations. For example, McLaughlin, Perosio and Park (1997) in their study of US retail logistics comment that 40 per cent of order fulfilment problems are a result of miscommunications between retail buyers and their own distribution centre personnel. However, they anticipate much greater use of technologies to the year 2000 with EDI exhibiting most growth (from 54 per cent of total company volume in 1996 to 88 per cent by 2000). In Europe, Walker (1994) showed that EDI usage was much greater in the United Kingdom than other European countries, notably Italy where the cost of telecommunications, a lack of management commitment and an insufficient critical mass of participants have left the Italians at the beginning of the adoption curve. Clearly, ECR initiatives on both sides of the Atlantic should lead to greater use of 'enabling technologies' and collaboration in the future.

As mentioned in Chapter 2, one area of collaboration that is often overlooked is that between retailer and professional logistics contractors. The provision of third party services to retailers varies markedly by country according to the regulatory environment, the competitiveness of the sector and other distribution 'culture' factors. For example, in the United Kingdom the deregulation of transport markets occurred in 1968 and many of the companies that provide dedicated distribution of RDCs today were the same companies that acted on behalf of suppliers when they controlled the supply chain 20 years ago. Retailers contracted out because of the opportunity cost of opening stores rather than RDCs, the cost was 'off balance sheet' and there was a cluster of well-established professional companies available to offer the service.

The situation is different in other geographical markets. In the United States, in particular, third party logistics is much less developed and warehousing is primarily run by the retailer whilst transportation is invariably contracted out to local haulers. Deregulation of transport markets has been relatively late in the United States, leading to more competitive pricing. Similarly, the progressive deregulation of EU markets is breaking down some nationally protected markets. Nevertheless, most European retailers, like their US counterparts, tend to only contract out the transport function. Compared with the United Kingdom, the economics of outsourcing is less attractive. Indeed, in some markets a strong balance sheet and the investment in distribution assets are viewed more positively than in the United Kingdom.

A TAXONOMY OF EUROPEAN GROCERY DISTRIBUTION NETWORKS

Commensurate with Fernie's (1994) observations on the eight major factors which account for differences in geographical markets, an attempt was made to cluster European countries according to a range of logistics-related variables. Eighteen variables were collected from a range of secondary data sources such as Eurostat publications, national trade association data, annual reports and management consultancy data. The variables were:

- area;
- road infrastructure;
  - road length
  - road density
- standard of living;

- population density;
- food outlet density;
- dominant trading format;
  — supermarket density
  — hypermarket density
  — discount share of domestic market
- own label penetration;
- food sales by organizational type;
  — multiples
  — co-ops
  — independents
- market share of top 5 grocers;
- development of IT;
- degree of overseas involvement;
- vertical channel integration;
  — turnover % from wholesalers
  — turnover % from manufacturers.

Initially it was intended to cover most European countries, but the lack of data from some countries narrowed down the choice to 10 EU countries. Furthermore, it was necessary to validate some of the data from a range of sources because of inconsistency in some data sets and definitional discrepancies. Nevertheless, it was possible to group the key variables into three sub-sets: market structure, trading format and physical/socio-economic.

Using the market structure data set as an example, the raw data are exhibited in Table 3.2 with the figures in parenthesis representing a standardization of the original values, for example, a large positive number signifies that the original number was large relative to the rest. After these data have been standardized, the Euclidean distance between pairs of countries can be calculated. Therefore Table 3.3 shows the squared Euclidean distance between pairs of countries whereby those countries with small squared distances (The Netherlands and France) would be expected to be grouped together compared with the United Kingdom and Portugal with high squared distances. By using the technique of cluster analysis and the average link algorithm, it was then possible to group the data for this data set and the others into country classifications.

Tables 3.4, 3.5 and 3.6 show the clusters and characteristics for each subgroup. The data do exhibit a broad north/south European split with Spain, Greece and Portugal being grouped together on most variables. Similarly, northern European countries cluster together although groupings invariably change according to each sub-set. Indeed, one has to be careful when interpreting the results. The United Kingdom and France are grouped together on many of the variables, especially the market structure and trading format data. However, although both countries have low food outlet densities, high multiple share of the market and a strong hypermarket/superstore presence, the markets are very different (see Fernie

Table 3.2 Matrix of variable values for market structure data

	Food Outlet Density	Multiples % of food market	Coops % of food market	Independents % of food markets	Own Label %	Market Share %
Belgium	144	32.7	1.0	66.3	18	40.0
B	−0.955	−0.417	−0.621	0.665	0.334	0.290
Denmark	292	37.0	21.0	42.0	18	29.6
DK	−0.371	−0.229	1.974	−0.439	0.334	−0.419
Germany	184	41.0	4.0	55.0	23	67.5
D	−0.797	−0.054	−0.232	0.151	0.897	2.168
Greece	542	45.0	0.0	55.0	na	26.0
GR	0.615	0.120	−0.751	0.151	−0.763	−0.665
Spain	515	35.0	1.8	63.2	7	36.2
E	0.508	−0.317	−0.517	0.524	−0.902	0.030
France	277	68.0	0.0	32.0	20	46.7
F	−0.430	1.128	−0.751	−0.894	0.559	0.747
Italy	586	10.0	17.0	73.0	7	22.1
I	0.788	−1.411	1.454	0.970	−0.902	−0.932
N'Lands	213	69.0	1.3	29.7	18	36.4
NL	−0.683	1.171	−0.582	−0.999	0.334	0.044
Portugal	935	10.0	1.0	89.0	1	14.4
P	2.166	−1.411	−0.621	1.562	−1.578	−1.458
UK	173	74.7	10.8	14.5	30	38.6
	−0.841	1.421	0.650	−1.691	1.685	0.194

Table 3.3 Squared Euclidean distance matrix: market structure data

		1	2	3	4	5	6	7	8	9
DK	2	8.84								
D	3	4.41	12.44							
GR	4	5.15	10.14	13.08						
E	5	3.78	9.65	9.80	0.90					
F	6	5.37	10.89	5.02	6.95	7.69				
IT	7	11.46	6.79	20.73	8.00	6.29	21.25			
NL	8	5.43	9.12	7.79	5.85	7.49	0.65	19.36		
P	9	18.25	23.32	32.04	8.05	7.70	28.68	7.29	27.27	
UK	10	12.40	8.46	10.87	15.90	17.84	4.42	26.38	3.93	42.65
		B	DK	D	GR	E	F	I	NL	P

and Pierrel, 1996 and Paché, 1995). Two of the largest French grocery retailers, Leclerc and Intermarché, are buying organizations with a large number of affiliated independent retailers. Buying structures are decentralized, own label penetration is low and there are numerous trading formats.

INTERNATIONALIZATION OF LOGISTICS PRACTICES

Although an analysis of these country markets does show differences in the factors which drive logistics practices, these markets are subject to much change. European retailers are seeking interna-

Table 3.4 Clusters and characteristics for market structure data

Cluster	Characteristics
Belgium, Germany	Low food outlet density, high discounters' share of food retailing, high own label.
Denmark, Italy	High co-ops and low multiples share of the food market.
Greece, Spain, Portugal	High food outlet density, low own label, low road density, low standard of living.
France, Netherlands, UK	Low food outlet density, high own label, high multiples share of the food market.

Table 3.5 Clusters and characteristics for trading format data

Cluster	Characteristics
Belgium, Germany, Denmark	High hypermarket density, high discounters' share of food retailing.
Greece	High supermarket density, low hypermarket density.
Italy, Portugal, Spain, Netherlands	Low hypermarket density.
France, UK	High hypermarket density.

Table 3.6 Clusters and characteristics for physical and socio-economic data

Cluster	Characteristics
Belgium, Netherlands	High road and population densities, high foreign involvement.
Denmark, Italy, UK, Germany	No important characteristics found.
Greece, Spain, Portugal	Low standard of living, low road and population densities, low foreign involvement.
France	Low population density, high area.

tional expansion, with the Spanish, Greek and Portuguese markets the target for development. This undoubtedly will lead to a transformation of market structures and trading formats as companies export their skills and concepts to new markets.

Clearly the transfer of 'know how', originally proposed by Kacker (1988) with reference to trading formats and concepts, can be applied to logistics practices. Indeed, we have shown already that Tesco and Sainsbury's acquisition strategy has led to a transformation of the logistics culture in these host markets. Alternatively, companies can pursue an organic growth strategy by building up a retail presence in target markets before rolling out an RDC support function. For example, Marks & Spencer's European retail strategy initially was supported from distribution centres in southern Britain. As French and Spanish markets were developed, warehouses were built to support these stores in Paris and Madrid, respectively. Another dimension to the internationalization of retail logistics is the internationalization of logistics service providers, many of whom were commissioned to operate sites on the basis of their relationship with retailers in the United Kingdom. In the above Marks & Spencer example, Exel Logistics is the contractor operating the DCs in France and Spain.

Another method of transferring 'know how' is through retail alliances. Throughout Europe, a large number of alliances exists, most of which are buying groups (Robinson and Clarke-Hill, 1995). However, some of these alliances have been promoting a cross-fertilization of logistics ideas and practices. In the case of the European Retail Alliance, Safeway in the United Kingdom has partnered Ahold of The Netherlands and Casino in France. In 1994 a 'composite' distribution centre was a UK phenomenon; now, composites have been developed by Safeway's European partners. These logistics practices have not only been applied in France and The Netherlands but in the parent companies' subsidiaries in the United States, Portugal and Czechoslovakia. Harvey (1997) comments that 'in the space of three years they caught up seven' (p. 6). Not surprisingly, the exploitation of UK retail logistics expertise has enabled distribution contractors to penetrate foreign retail markets, not only in support of British retail companies, entry strategies but for other international retailers. Harvey (1997) argues that the success of his company (Tibbett & Britten) and other UK logistics specialists can be derived from the success of the fast-moving consumer goods sector but, like UK retailers, the success for the future lies with global opportunities.

REFERENCES

Akehurst, G and Alexander, N. (1996) *The Internationalisation of Retailing*, Frank Cass, London

Alexander, N (1997) *International Retailing*, Blackwell Publishers, Oxford

Christopher, M (1997) *Marketing Logistics*, Butterworth-Heinemann, Oxford

Cooper, J (1993) *Reconfiguring European Logistics*, Council of Logistics Management, Chicago

Coopers & Lybrand (1996) *European Value Chain Analysis Study – Final Report*, ECR Europe, Utrecht

Corporate Intelligence on Retailing (1998) Strategic issues in retailing – an aide memoire for management, *1998 Retail Week Conference*, London

Davis, M (1995) *The Future Distribution: Strategies for Success in a Changing Industry*, FT Management Report, Pearson, London.

Fernie, J (1994) Quick Response: an international perspective, *International Journal of Physical Distribution and Logistics Management*, 24(6), pp 38–46

Fernie, J (1995) International comparisons of supply chain management in grocery retailing, *Service Industries Journal*, 15(4), pp 134–47

Fernie, J and Pierrel, FRA (1996) Own branding in UK and French grocery markets, *Journal of Product and Brand Management*, 5(3), pp 48–57

Fiddis, C (1997) *Manufacturer–Retailer Relationships in the Food and Drink Industry: Strategies and Tactics in the Battle for Power*; FT Retail and Consumer Publishing, Pearson Professional, London

GEA Consultia (1994) *Supplier-Retailer Collaboration in Supply Chain Management*, Coca-Cola Retailing Research Group Europe, London

Harland, DA (1994) Achieving a global business, the role of logistics, *Logistics Focus*, 2(7), pp 2–7

Harvey, J (1997) International contract logistics, *Logistics Focus*, April, pp 2–6

Holmes, G (1995) *Supply Chain Management: Europe's New Competitive Battleground*, Economic Intelligence Unit, London

Kacker, M (1988) International flows of retail know-how: bridging the technology gap in distributions, *Journal of Retailing*, 64(1), pp 41–67

Machel, PG (1993) Supply chain strategy in a multinational environment, paper presented at the IGD Conference, *Improving Supply Chain Effectiveness in the Grocery Trade*, London, February

McLaughlin, EW, Perosio, DJ and Park, JL (1997) *Retail Logistics and Merchandising: Requirements in the Year 2000*, Cornell University, Ithaca, New York

Mitchell, A (1997) *Efficient Consumer Response: A New Paradigm for the European FMCG Sector*, FT Retail and Consumer Publishing, Pearson Professional, London.

Ohbora, T, Parsons, A and Riesenbeck, H (1992) Alternative routes to global marketing, *The McKinsey Quarterly*, 3, pp 52–74

Paché, G (1995) Speculative inventories in the food retailing industry: a comment on French practices, *International Journal of Retail and Distribution Management*, 23(12), pp 36–42

Peck, H and Christopher, M (1994) Laura Ashley: the logistics challenge, in *Cases in Retail Management*, ed P McGoldrick, pp 310–23, Pitman, London

Robinson, T and Clarke-Hill, C.M (1995) International alliances in European retailing, in *International Retailing Trade and Strategies*, ed PJ McGoldrick and G Davies, Pitman, London

Shaw, SA, Dawson, JA and Blair, LMA (1992) Imported foods in a British supermarket chain, *International Review of Retail, Distribution and Consumer Research*, 2(1), pp 35–57

Sparks, L (1995) Reciprocal retail internationalisation: the Southland Corporation, Ito-Yokado and 7-Eleven Convenience Stores, *Service Industries Journal*, 15(4), pp 57–96

Sternquist, B (1998) *International Retailing*, Fairchild Books, New York

St. Quentin, (1993) *Trends in European Logistics Activity*, St Quentin, London

Walker, M (1994) Supplier-retailer collaboration in European grocery distribution, paper presented at an IGD Conference 'Profitable Collaboration in Supply Chain Management', London

Wrigley, N (1997a) British food retail capital in the USA – Part 1: Sainsbury and the Shaws experience, *International Journal of Retail and Distribution Management*, 25(1), pp 7–21

Wrigley, N (1997b) British food retail capital in the USA – Part 2: Giant prospects, *International Journal of Retail and Distribution Management*, 25(2), pp 48–58

4

TAKING COALS TO NEWCASTLE: THE MOVEMENT OF CLOTHING TO HONG KONG AND THE FAR EAST

Paul Jackson

INTRODUCTION

Marks and Spencer has been doing rather well in an area of the world that is noted for its clothing exports rather than its clothing imports. How has this happened, and why was it necessary to carry out a major overhaul of the way Marks & Spencer moves clothing and food 10 000 miles to Hong Kong? To understand the logistics operation in the Far East, it is necessary to provide some background to Hong Kong to illustrate some of the reasons for the Marks and Spencer growth in Southeast Asia.

Hong Kong occupies a central position in Asia with nearly all major Asian cities within a four-hour flight radius (see Figure 4.1). Its territory is made up of a mainland peninsula, Kowloon and the New Territories, and over 230 outlying islands, as well as Hong Kong Island itself. Its only natural resource is its deep-water port. All raw materials are imported and agriculture occupies a minor part of Hong Kong life, 9 per cent of the land area and only 2 per cent of the labour market. Most of the foodstuffs such as rice, vegetables,

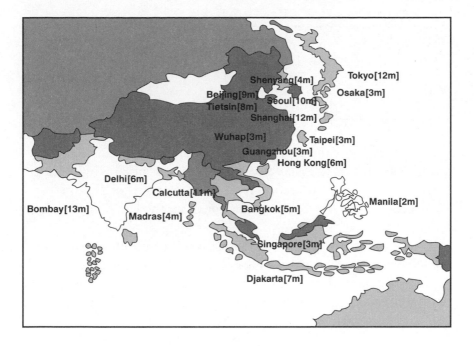

Figure 4.1 Principal cities in Asia

poultry, meat and even water are imported from China. Only in fish is there a high degree of self-sufficiency. The climate is sub-tropical with hot, humid summers, wet autumns and cool winters. Apart from the tropical storms and typhoons it can be pleasant at other times!

Hong Kong's population, 98 per cent of whom are Chinese, has increased since the end of the war and is as shown in Table 4.1. Hong Kong is one of the most tightly packed cities of the world, with 95 per cent living in the densely populated urban areas. And yet, in contrast, there are many islands, and parts of the New Territories, which are very sparsely populated.

Historically, Britain has been involved in the area since Victorian times, as the Island of Hong Kong was ceded to the United Kingdom, in perpetuity, in 1842. Kowloon was added subsequently. The New Territories were leased from China in 1898 for

Table 4.1 Increase in population of Hong Kong, 1945–96

Year	Population
1945	600 000
1950	2 200 000
1970	4 000 000
1996	6 300 000

99 years (see Figure 4. 2). It was felt by the Thatcher administration that Kowloon and the Island would not be sustainable without the New Territories, so an accord with China was negotiated in 1984. This accord arranged for the handover of all the land back to China in 1997.

Economically, life in Hong Kong was not good until the mid-1960s. Penury and squalor were the norm prior to the economy taking off. By the mid-1970s, however, it had emerged as one of the great trading nations of the world. In 1995, Hong Kong exported US$151 billion worth of products, which made it the eighth largest exporter in the world. It has one of the largest global stock markets

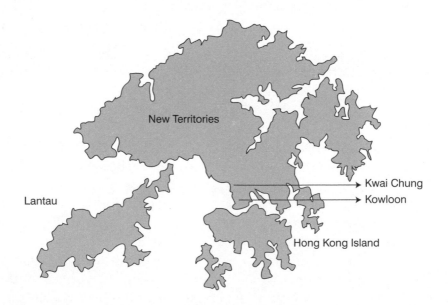

Figure 4.2 Map of Hong Kong and the New Territories

with a capitalization of more than US$35.5 billion, and 85 of the world's top banks are represented in Hong Kong.

This growth in the economy has resulted in a growth in retailing – it now has developed a worldwide reputation as a retail centre catering for both the traditional outdoor markets as well as some of the most prestigious shopping malls. The bulk of this upmarket activity has hitherto been in the Central Causeway Bay areas on the Island and in Kowloon; however, there has been a recent trend in retail development in the new townships such as Shatin.

MARKS AND SPENCER IN HONG KONG

The Marks and Spencer operation in Hong Kong started out in the classically new entry mode with a franchise partner, Dodwells, who sold the company's St Michael brand products for many years in its shops. The sales growth was satisfactory and a clear market for these goods was beginning to emerge.

At the same time, and coincidentally, by the latter part of the 1980s the company was starting to source more of its buying in the Far East. Many of the company's manufacturers were beginning to produce goods in the emerging 'Tiger' economic states of Taiwan, Singapore and Hong Kong. Additionally, Sri Lanka and the Philippines were also emerging as potential manufacturing bases. Several of the Hong Kong and Japanese companies were beginning to open production plants in China and using Hong Kong as their exporting point. Japan had, by now, become increasingly important to Marks and Spencer as a provider of high quality fabric, in particular the so-called polyester 'silks'.

As many of the company's buyers and technologists were therefore spending an increasing amount of time in the Far East, clearly an excessive amount of travelling was involved. As it was envisaged that these demands were likely to expand, a strategic decision was made to establish a buying and technological base in Hong Kong to serve the entire area.

Subsequent to this, and as a result of the global expansion of the business, it was decided that the time was right to launch a subsidiary company in Hong Kong, and thus Marks and Spencer amicably ended its agreement with Dodwells. Lord Rayner, Chairman, 1984–90, commented on the 'exciting aspects that this would give the business towards the Millennium'. He was determined to pursue a policy of global expansion for the company. The prestigious menswear retailer, Brooks Brothers, was purchased in the United States. Later, a US supermarket chain, Kings, was also acquired. In Europe, the expansion into new countries, either as subsidiaries, such as in Spain, or franchise operations, such as in Portugal and Greece, gathered momentum. The objective was to initiate 'the development of a truly mainstream volume retail business in all the countries where we trade and to initially cluster stores in metropolitan areas to achieve efficiencies of scale' (Company Report 1995).

Those early days in Hong Kong were not without their traumas. One of the first stores, at Mong Kok, was closed after a short time, but from these tentative beginnings the business has grown rapidly. By 1995 there were seven stores – five on the island of Hong Kong – the largest of the stores at the Ocean Centre Terminal in Kowloon, and one store deep in the New Territories at Shatin. Substantial sums have been allocated to international growth and the development of systems to facilitate this growth.

The sales increases have been tremendous, with large increases being made throughout the 1990s, typically around 30 per cent growth each year. Current sales are well in excess of HK$1.2 billion and sales increases have continued throughout the handover period of the erstwhile colony to China. Sales per square foot (the method of comparison still used by this traditional company) and profitability are among the highest in the company.

Additional stores have opened and it is envisaged that there could be as many as 15 stores in total in the area by moving into traditional Hong Kong Chinese neighbourhoods. The company has opened another five stores during the last two years and more are in the pipeline, with a predicted sales growth of three times the 1995 level. As an office was established in China in 1995, it is likely that the company will move into areas such as Guangzhou, Shanghai and Beijing.

Some interesting sales comparisons are that Hong Kong stores take more money on toiletries than Marble Arch, the company's flagship store, and three times more than most UK stores. In the sale of ladieswear, the Hong Kong stores are second only to Marble Arch for their voracious appetite in purchasing the blouses and skirts that are the bedrock of the Marks and Spencer offer.

The stores in Hong Kong are all in modern air-conditioned malls and are typically smaller than in the UK (see Figure 4.3). This gives them a distinctive flavour which, as a result of their more intimate size, is a cross between a boutique and a small departmental store. The many floors further enhance this image, which gives a 'small shop' ambience. An exclusive and expensive carrier bag is but a small part of the Hong Kong marketing offer, which adds a plus to the selling offer.

In spite of the above differences, they are still very clearly Marks and Spencer stores with browsing, 'no hassle' refunds, and self-selection which helps to keep the costs low. Premise rental in Hong Kong for all sectors is very expensive and is usually more costly than labour!

Figure 4.3 Marks and Spencer's seventh store in Hong Kong

The cataloguing policy is to offer a wide range of 'upmarket' goods similar to those which would be found in the company's stores in London or Paris. Prices are considerably higher than in the United Kingdom, but Marks and Spencer is perceived as a premium brand, reflecting the quality of the goods rather than the equivalent market position in the United Kingdom or the United States; these prices are, however, lower than the local 'designer' clothes shops. The British connection still carries a cachet that is unlikely to be lost as a symbol for reliability and quality.

The fascination of the Hong Kong retail environment is the sheer unpredictability of the market. Many of the goods sold are being bought for resale elsewhere, as the amount of bulk sales is always high. These large purchases have to be taken into account when considering replenishment options.

Approximately 10 per cent of the merchandise is locally sourced, although local means anywhere in the Far East buying region; this can mean merchandise from such diverse areas as Sri Lanka or Mauritius as well as Hong Kong. The only true local merchandise is 'Asian Fit Bras', as the standard UK sizes are not reflective of the silhouette of the Hong Kong population.

The Marks and Spencer Asian Pacific Head office is based at the Ocean Centre in Kowloon and employs some 80 people. These include some expatriates, headed by a main Board Director and two Divisional Directors. It would be wrong to give the impression that all of these are purely involved in the Hong Kong operation, as this office also looks after the extensive Far East franchise business, in addition to some aspects of the buying operation for the main group.

HONG KONG SUPPLY CHAIN AND WAREHOUSING OPERATION

The warehousing for this operation is located deeper in Kowloon at Kwai Chung. It is located in one of the world's largest buildings, ATL, which has over 4 million square feet of warehouse space. A remarkable building, bigger than the Pentagon, it features a six-lane highway in and out of the warehouse. The Marks and Spencer site occupies some 41 000 square feet (gross) and is contracted to one of the M&S third party 'partners', Exel Logistics (see Figure 4.4).

The logistical problems facing the Hong Kong business in 1995

Many logistical problems were highlighted, and the following is a brief summation of the major areas of concern:

- Consistent volume growth-business had quadrupled in 3 years with the consequent problems that this brought to the structure.
- Business was expected to double yet again by 1999.
- Despatch points in the United Kingdom had changed.
- Hong Kong warehouse had recently been resited, together with the decision to outsource the responsibility for the operation to Exel Logistics. This is the normal approach within the UK business but was new for Hong Kong. Exel also are responsible for some of the other overseas operations such as warehousing in France and Spain. This change had resulted in some initial 'teething' problems which would require some attention.

Figure 4.4 The ATL Building at Kwai Chung

- Air freight capacity had come under pressure; it was frequently difficult to pre-book flight space and sometimes goods were not transported.
- Air freight charges had increased, and reflected the volume space that the company was using on the freighters and not the actual weight of the garments. This was to play an important part in looking at the longer-term resolution of the supply chain.
- Systems to effect the storage and movement were in the main manual, being both labour and space consumptive, and had not changed significantly from the initial set-up in Hong Kong.
- Stock holdings, the amount of stock that was being held in Hong Kong, had increased, and stock turnover had fallen to 3.5 times per year; and this in spite of increased sales levels! Some of this increase was due to poor transit/shipping time, and an increasing amount of storage of locally produced stock.
- Inventory accuracy was poor; delivery documentation was often inadequate.
- Costs were escalating and service levels were being affected as the third party contractors found it difficult to manage the demands expected by the customer.

The resulting impact of the above was to push the supply chain into near collapse; the inefficencies were only too evident at every stage of the chain. It would require major changes to regain control of the costs, which had begun to spiral upwards. The above were a contributory factor in inhibiting the introduction of new IT systems. These included the use of Electronic Data Interchange (EDI) links with central headquarters and the introduction of a new goods management system.

THE UNITED KINGDOM TO HONG KONG SUPPLY CHAIN

Figure 4.5 shows the points where the stock destined for sale in Hong Kong actually touches en route. It assumes that a delivery instruction to a supplier has originated from the UK Head Office. The merchandise follows the exact route of the UK supply chain in that it follows the supply chain through the primary consolidation points, for foods, hanging garments or boxed stock. The primary chain is so called as it enables consolidation of stock to be achieved, thus optimizing lorry usage.

Foods are delivered to one of the Marks and Spencer Food Depots which specialize in export, and all non-foods are delivered to a special section of one of the general merchandise warehouses. Here the goods are checked, booked in for record purposes and prepared for onward transportation to Hong Kong.

The goods were then loaded onto specially constructed light-weight frames. These frames had to conform to the aircraft footprints and as the organization used 747 freighters these were designed to maximize the space. However, as shall be discussed later, these frames were grossly inefficient as the relationship of weight/volume moved was poor. These were so designed as to obviate any additional preparation at the Hong Kong warehouse, such as ironing and rehanging of hanging garments, all of which come into the Marks and Spencer distribution system already hung and ready for sales floor presentation. In the main, all garments were, and still are, delivered by air. Toiletries and foods are delivered by sea.

Figure 4.6 shows the time that it was actually taking to get goods out onto the Hong Kong sales floor. From the time of allocation it was, on average, taking some 22 days for stock to arrive on the sales floor in Hong Kong. Some stock was even taking up to 27 days, and this using air transport! One of the first tasks was to establish why this was so; some of the reasons why there were these considerable time delays are as follows:

- Flight delays – aircraft can be delayed, and have several drop off or pick up points en route. However, in the main, most journeys – 99 per cent – were always completed within a 24-hour time frame. Whilst this could be a contributory factor, it was not where the real problems lay; yet it was the one most quoted as

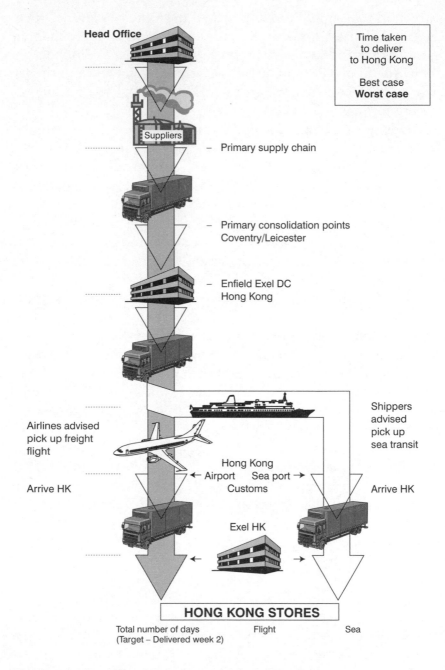

Figure 4.5 UK to Hong Kong logistical flow diagram 1

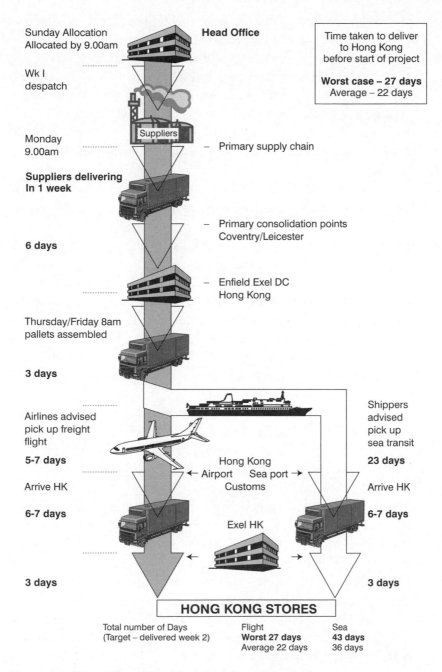

Sunday Allocation
Allocated by 9.00am

Head Office

Time taken to deliver
to Hong Kong
before start of project

Worst case – 27 days
Average – 22 days

Wk I
despatch

Monday
9.00am

Suppliers

– Primary supply chain

**Suppliers delivering
In 1 week**

– Primary consolidation points
Coventry/Leicester

6 days

– Enfield Exel DC
Hong Kong

Thursday/Friday 8am
pallets assembled

3 days

Airlines advised
pick up freight
flight

Shippers
advised
pick up
sea transit

5-7 days

Hong Kong
← Airport   Sea port →
Customs

23 days

Arrive HK

Arrive HK

6-7 days

Exel HK

6-7 days

3 days

3 days

HONG KONG STORES

| Total number of Days (Target – delivered week 2) | Flight **Worst 27 days** Average 22 days | Sea **43 days** 36 days |

Figure 4.6 UK to Hong Kong logistical flow diagram 2

the reason for delays. It was easy to attribute blame to factors outside the normal span of control.

- Export stock not always receiving priority, contrary to the company's instructions to suppliers, which specify that all overseas goods should be despatched from suppliers prior to outloading UK requirements.
- Stock awaiting transportation at UK depots – this could take up to five days before the airline handling agents picked up the frames.
- Use of different airlines – some journeys would go via Amsterdam which would add up to three days as goods were moved from the United Kingdom to Holland.
- Hong Kong airport – Kai Tak – delays at this point were due, in part, to the choice of the initial carrier. Cathay Pacific were the only airline at that time to offer a 24-hour, 7-days a week cargo handling system. All others – the company were using four different airlines – did not operate outside of the normal business hours, five days a week. The consequence of this was that any deliveries that arrived after 17.00 hours had to wait until 9.00 the following day prior to being released from the cargo area. This was exacerbated over the course of a weekend. A Friday night landing at 17.00 was not processed until Monday and storage charges had to be paid for the weekend!
- Handling agents – it is necessary to use handling agents to enable goods to be released from Kai Tak. Again, these agents were only picking up stock from the airport during the week. Unnecessary expense was being incurred at the airport by having to pay for this overnight or weekend storage. Mondays were therefore very busy days and frequently goods would not surface until Tuesday. The handling agents were also badly selected in that they did not appreciate the size and scale of Marks and Spencer demands. The liaison between the agents and the warehouse was poor. For example, the warehouse could not cope with the surges of stock at the beginning of the week and secondary storage of goods was common in godowns. (A godown is a vertical warehousing facility; as land is so expensive, this

form of storage is the cheapest available. It is restrictive in the sense that it is usually reliant on a single lift to operate several floors!) This not only added to the expense but increased the delays. Another interesting problem was the airport's insistence on receiving cash, as the agents were not themselves large enough to warrant credit. And Marks and Spencer is the only Triple AAA rated retailer ranked by Moody and Poors in the world! This created further delays to the process.

- Warehouse – much work needed to be done at this end. The warehouse had been in operation for six months and there was a credibility gap between the local Marks and Spencer management and the then warehouse management. For example, order and space needed to be created in order to create an operational environment which would enable a workflow for the accurate reception, storage and despatch to the stores. Goods would not be dealt with immediately on arrival and delays due to booking-in errors were frequent and time-consuming.

In spite of these problems, or perhaps because of them, there was a willingness and a realization that changes were necessary and that there would have to be some instant solutions as well as a longer-term perspective to the review. It was necessary to establish some 'quick wins' to energize the project and create a climate of change.

The issues, though multi-faceted, had to be addressed not only in Hong Kong but also in the United Kingdom. The first action was to analyse every aspect of the supply chain from the collection of sales data in Hong Kong, the allocation of new stock, how it was to be despatched, to its receipt in the Hong Kong warehouse and preparation for display on the sales floors of the Hong Kong stores.

Second, an action plan for immediate, medium-term and long-term solutions was to be constructed and agreed with all involved parties. Third, the implementation of some of the proposed solutions would be put into action at the same time as the development of the long-term plans. These would need to be discussed and agreed with all the players. Because of the distances, and the problems that these would give, implementation would only be considered if there was a cost benefit to any actions.

As can be seen from the flow plan (Figure 4.6), every point of the supply chain needed to be looked at, as there was time lost at each stage of the process. As there were more issues at the Hong Kong end of the chain, which were more amenable to immediate only action, it was decided to start at this juncture, in order to get some 'quick wins'.

Service levels were examined and agreed with the Hong Kong management team. Immediate steps were then taken to keep to these. For example, every store had two deliveries every day irrespective of size or need. Whilst this was appropriate for the major units, it was an unrealistic imposition for the warehouse to provide the smaller stores with this level of service. The stores were having to order stock every few hours and were constantly spending time on this function and not on customer service or selling activities.

In a similar manner, one of the major concerns of the stores was the soilage of many of the garments arriving into the shops from the warehouse. It was clear that a factor in this was the removal, at the warehouse, of the protective polythene wrapping from the garments. This was compounded by two other influences – that of very poor and dirty shared reception facilities at the shopping malls, and the dusty, grimy traffic conditions. These were due to the major construction works occasioned by the new airport infrastructure. As these works were adjacent to Kwai Chung, it was inevitable that this would affect the condition of the goods.

By altering the amount of deliveries into the stores, and by leaving the garment bags on the goods, service levels were actually improved at the same time as cutting costs. Once all parties realized that there was a 'win-win' syndrome about the review, more radical actions were able to be initiated. The warehouse management had to learn that saying 'yes' to requests from a variety of customers would impinge not only on service levels to the others, it would add to costs and possibly confuse the warehouse staff!

A series of meetings to review the time that it was taking the goods to arrive at the warehouse were set up in Hong Kong. Discussions were initiated with the airport handling agents, the airport authorities, the airlines, the commercial managers of the stores, and above all, with the warehouse management.

Some 500 actions were identified, and measures were set in train to initiate some of these. The first action was to re-lay the warehouse to allow more operational space. This was achieved by examining all the goods that were being held in the warehouse and being ruthless with any non-essential activity. For example, equipment for the stores, old tills, display equipment, bags and rubbish were all taking up space which was needed for core activities. Private cars were being parked in loading bays which was preventing access to the reception and dispatch of goods. Old aircraft frames from the flights were being left until an intermittent disposal arrangement was activated. An immediate action was to clear these away from the operational areas. Unsatisfactory goods, which were normally returned to the manufacturers, were being stored prior to disposing to charity, often up to six months at a time and thus taking up valuable space in the warehouse. A regular weekly collection by the recipients was arranged, who were only too happy to do so.

Once the operational space was obtained, an in-depth look was undertaken to establish how goods were being booked into the warehouse. Improvements were made which resulted in this feature being speeded up. This resulted in smoothing the operation to the extent that the dwell-time was reduced by two-thirds. There were many other such examples and these had to be addressed in a holistic way, so as to retain a 'helicopter vision' of the sum of the proposed improvements.

By involving the handling agents in some of the discussions and inviting them to the Baker Street headquarters, it was possible to start and inculcate the values that the company aspires to in its dealings with its suppliers. Clear instructions and procedures were arranged, credit facilities were explored and the company was able to facilitate a meeting with the airport handlers which was most satisfactory. Where possible, flights would only be booked that would arrive in Hong Kong airport's working windows; the handling agent would pick up on weekends and deliver to the warehouse. This was to save considerable sums in storage charges as well as easing the warehouse work schedule. The net result of this work with the handling agents and the Kai Tak authorities was a saving in time of up to six days which could be taken out of the time spent in transit of the stock – this was a considerable improvement.

The airlines were professional and able to respond to reasonable requests that took cognisance of their restraints and abilities. By careful resheduling of the flight patterns, savings were easy to achieve and a quicker response time was initiated and achieved. This resulted in the stores being able to order stock within 24 hours of the stock landing in Hong Kong (see Figure 4.7).

ACTION IN THE UNITED KINGDOM

At the UK end of the supply chain it was necessary to adopt a more considered and less immediate approach. A letter was sent to all suppliers reminding them of the need to send overseas goods first, which was received and acted upon. This did produce results and was instrumental in taking another few days' delay out of the delivery time. Time was spent trawling through the supply chain operation within the United Kingdom to see if there were any other areas of possible time savings. It was quickly established that there were no savings to be had during the transit times of the goods through the primary chain. However, whilst the booking-in procedures were excellent at the UK despatch point, there were some savings that could be made in the collection and dispatch to Heathrow or Amsterdam.

It also became apparent that not only were the reception procedures excellent but there was an additional process as the goods were also recorded and booked into Hong Kong. The booking-in procedures in Hong Kong gave rise to a number of queries as the space restrictions alluded to earlier did not make for an easy operating area, and a lack of scanning equipment meant that the manual procedures were more prone to errors. It was proposed, and

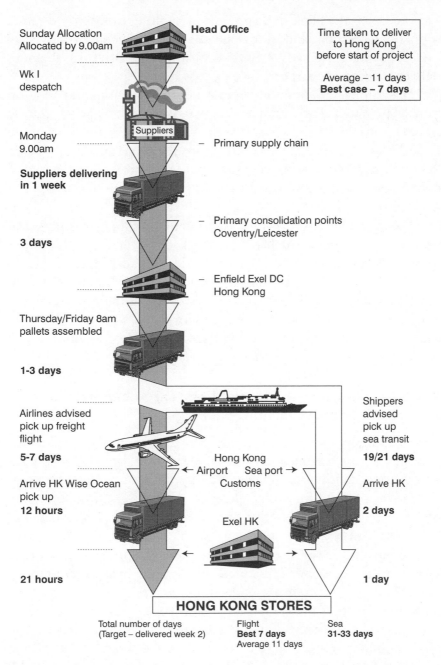

Sunday Allocation
Allocated by 9.00am

Head Office

Time taken to deliver
to Hong Kong
before start of project

Average – 11 days
Best case – 7 days

Wk I
despatch

Monday
9.00am

Suppliers

– Primary supply chain

**Suppliers delivering
in 1 week**

3 days

– Primary consolidation points
  Coventry/Leicester

– Enfield Exel DC
  Hong Kong

Thursday/Friday 8am
pallets assembled

1-3 days

Airlines advised
pick up freight
flight

Shippers
advised
pick up
sea transit

5-7 days

Hong Kong
← Airport   Sea port →
Customs

19/21 days

Arrive HK Wise Ocean
pick up
12 hours

Arrive HK

Exel HK

2 days

21 hours

1 day

HONG KONG STORES

Total number of days
(Target – delivered week 2)

Flight
Best 7 days
Average 11 days

Sea
31-33 days

Figure 4.7 UK to Hong Kong logistical flow diagram 3

accepted, that the booking-in operation in Hong Kong would cease, suppliers would be paid as a result of the goods being received in the UK warehouse, which was a positive incentive to them to deliver their goods earlier.

This implementation did necessitate some spending on an additional IT system. For example, the provision of scanners, and the installation of EDI links with Hong Kong to alert the warehouse and the stores that goods had been received and were being despatched. However, the cost savings in the warehouse equated to over HK$1.2million, as well as speeding the operation by saving yet another day!

The moral here is that it is easy to get into a 'non-trusting' relationship; the same third party contractor was booking the goods into the Marks and Spencer system in the United Kingdom. Half a world away, the same company was unpacking these sealed containers packed by their colleagues and repeating the process manually. Any mistakes – and there were many, perceived or real – were subject to an industry of faxes and secondary checks, all of which delayed the sales of the goods.

Visits to other industries, suppliers, cargo handlers and the introduction of vacuum packing

It was apparent that the airframes that the company were using, although fit for the purpose, were a very costly option if the business was to continue sending goods by air freight. Investigations were carried out to find some alternatives and to achieve a method of intensifying the stock sent to the Far East in less space than was being used. At the same time, it was not an option that the goods should have to be reprocessed, for example, re-pressed, when they arrived in Hong Kong. This ruled out options such as 'cramming' goods into boxes and thus gaining stock intensity and another common method, that of 'hanging' knotted ropes from the ceiling of containers thus utilizing all the space within it. Both of these methods required merchandise to be resuscitated at the final destination and that in itself required space, time and resources.

Vacuum packing of merchandise

One of the Marks and Spencer suppliers, Dewhirst, had opened a blouse factory in Malacca, Malaysia. Dewhirst also happened to be its oldest supplier, as it was the first company to supply Michael Marks, the founder of Marks and Spencer, with his first trays of harberdashery. They had carried out an experiment with a Hong Kong company, Vac Pac, in order to investigate the possibilities of more efficient transportation back to the United Kingdom. Goods were made as normal, pressing and hanging were finished, and the garments were overbagged with polythene. The garments were then subjected to some special treatments. First, they were put into a dehumidifying chamber for a period, which extracted the moisture from the garments. It had been established that only garments with a moisture content are susceptible to creasing. Garments that are ultra dry can be folded, stacked and pressed, providing that they remain free from moisture, and will retain the shape that they were in prior to the dehumidification. After this all the air is extracted from the garments by placing an overbag around the garments and utilizing a suction process. The garments are then packed tightly into boxes. This principle had already been used by Marks and Spencer for the sale of its duvets and pillows in its stores since the late 1980s.

The garments thus packed would take up less room and be more space-efficient. When they arrived at their destination, they would, after a brief period of recovery, rehumidify, and be ready for sale without recourse to extra preparation at the receiving end. This experiment had not worked as the sole machinery to perform this operation was in Hong Kong, some four hours away. It would have been, in Dewhirst's view, too costly to implement or to purchase the machinery for installation in Malaysia. When investigations were initiated it was established that there was a UK agent for the process, and Vac Pac themselves were situated directly under the Hong Kong warehouse at Kwai Chung. On visiting the Vac Pac operation in Hong Kong, it was obvious that if the quality standards could be achieved, then it could have a positive impact in reducing the costs of the movement of goods not just to Hong Kong, but anywhere else that the business was selling goods, either the subsidiaries such as Canada or the many franchises throughout the world.

Extensive tests were carried out by packing goods in Hong Kong, sending them to the United Kingdom and then sending them back again! It was found that, with one or two exceptions, the merchandise was perfect when it reached the sales floors of the Hong Kong stores. The exceptions were those garments which had themselves, as part of the manufacturing process, undergone some form of heat treatment, such as non-iron shirts. These were not able to be transported by this method, thus the alternatives had to be kept for these.

The decision was made to go ahead with the Vac Pac operation, as it was envisaged that there would potentially be enormous cost benefits. Machinery has been installed in the United Kingdom to perform this during 1996–97 and the savings are currently in excess of £1 million per annum. As the volume grows, so too will the savings, and as the other countries are included savings will accrue.

CONCLUSIONS

There can never be a substitute for 'on the spot', 'management by walking about' visits and probing. No matter how isolated subsidiaries are, they need the input of experts to ensure that 'best practices' are properly promulgated and implemented on a regular and ongoing basis. Cost reduction and, more importantly, time reduction, were achieved. The local management quickly bought into the changes once they were assured that the 'quick wins' which had been delivered were for their benefit and would have longevity – a classic win-win situation.

It is always difficult to predict the future – the only thing that is predictable is usually change! However, if the company's growth is sustained in the region, then there are a number of additional scenarios which will further reduce the company's costs. These will present both it and its suppliers with a number of lower cost options and enhanced commercial opportunities.

These could include the company setting up a major distribution centre in the Far East which could act as a hub for all merchandise flowing from and to all parts of the Marks and Spencer empire. Manufacturers would place their goods here prior to onward dispatch to wherever the goods are required for sale. UK production destined for sale in the region will be centrally stored, thus gaining some economies of scale and the ability to have, if necessary, a secondary distribution system closer to the point of sale.

Once this is established, then the future direction is obvious and achievable. The company should then charter its own aircraft. This would then be the most efficient, cost-effective and certain method of establishing and keeping control of both time and costs. Manufacturers would be able to 'backload' to the United Kingdom, thus ensuring full usage.

DISCLAIMER

This document describes the author's experiences when he was working in the Far East, and does not represent the official views of Marks and Spencer plc.

5

FASHION LOGISTICS

Martin Christopher and Helen Peck

INTRODUCTION

The ability to respond to customer requirements on a timely basis has always been a fundamental element of the marketing concept. However, there has perhaps never been as much pressure as exists today to accelerate further the responsiveness of marketing systems. 'Time-based competition' has become the norm in many markets from banking to automobiles. The challenge to marketing and logistics in the current environment is to find ways in which product development times can be reduced, feedback from the market-place made more rapid and replenishment times compressed.

Nowhere is this pressure more evident than in markets governed by fashion. Fashion is a broad term which typically encompasses any product or market where there is an element of style which is likely to be short-lived. We have defined fashion markets as exhibiting typically the following characteristics:

1. Short life-cycles – the product is often ephemeral, designed to capture the mood of the moment; consequently, the period in which it is saleable is likely to be very short and seasonal, measured in months or even weeks.

2. High volatility – demand for these products is rarely stable or linear. It may be influenced by the vagaries of weather, hit films, TV shows or even indirectly by advertising. Julia Roberts' appearance in the film *Pretty Woman* wearing a brown and white polka dot dress cleared the shops of similar dresses, and a Volkswagen advertisement featuring a newly divorced woman in a white top hat sent millinery sales soaring.
3. Low predictability – because of the volatility of demand it is extremely difficult to forecast with any accuracy even total demand during a period, let alone week-by-week or market-by-market requirements.
4. High impulse purchase – many buying decisions for these products are made at the point of purchase. In other words, the shopper when confronted with the product is stimulated to buy it, hence the critical role of 'availability' and, in particular, availability of sizes, colours, etc.

The combined effect of these pressures clearly provides a challenge to logistics management. Traditional ways of responding to customer demand have been forecast-based, with the resultant risk of over-stocked or under-stocked situations.

More recently there has emerged another trend that has added further complexity and difficulty to the management of fashion logistics. The growing tendency to source product and materials off-shore has led in many cases to significantly longer lead-times. Whilst there is usually a substantial cost advantage to be gained, particularly in manufacturing, through sourcing in low labour cost areas, the effect on lead-times can be severe. It is not only distance that causes replenishment lead-times to lengthen in global sourcing. It is the delays and variability caused by internal processes at both ends of the chain as well as the import/export procedures in between. The end result is longer 'pipelines' with more inventory in them, with the consequent risks of obsolescence that arise.

Much of the pressure for seeking low-cost manufacturing

solutions has come from retailers. Between 1986 and 1991 one-sixth of all clothing factories in the European Union closed down as retailers switched their sourcing off-shore, increasingly to the Far East (Fitzpatrick, 1994).

At the same time there have been moves by many retailers in the apparel business to reduce significantly the number of suppliers they do business with. This supply-base rationalization has been driven by a number of considerations, but in particular by the need to develop more responsive replenishment systems – something that is not possible when sourcing is spread over hundreds, if not thousands, of suppliers.

Two extracts from Annual Reports of the Burton Group plc highlight this trend:

> By trading with fewer suppliers, we are in a better position to leverage our purchasing power and buy more competitively. More importantly, by working in close partnership with manufacturers we are able to make the supply chain far more responsive to the demands of the market ... Stronger supplier relationships play an essential role in this move by enabling us to call off extra orders at short notice to maintain the right balance of stock.
>
> (Burton Group plc, 1994)

> Rapid stock replenishment is vital to our business, where fashion trends can change by the month ... To maintain our fashion edge throughout the seasons, we have worked to reduce our lead times and increase the flexibility of our supply chain. Today, we are dealing with less than half the number of suppliers compared to two years ago, with the top twenty responsible for over three-quarters of our business. Some 70 per cent of manufacture now takes place in Europe, enabling us to receive repeat orders in as little as three weeks.
>
> (Burton Group plc, 1995)

MANAGING THE FASHION LOGISTICS PIPELINE

Conventional wisdom holds that the way to cope with uncertainty is to improve the quality of the forecast. Yet, by definition, the volatility of demand and the short life cycles found in many fashion markets make it highly unlikely that forecasting methods will ever be developed that can consistently and accurately predict sales at the item level. Instead, ways must be found of reducing the reliance that organizations place upon the forecast and instead they must focus on lead-time reduction. Shorter lead times mean, by definition, that the forecasting horizon is shorter – hence the risk of error is lower. In the same way that the captain of a super-tanker has a planning horizon that is determined by the vessel's stopping distance (many miles), so too in business the forecast period is determined by the time it takes to design, make and ship the product – lead times, in other words.

There are three critical lead times that must be managed by organizations that seek to compete successfully in fashion markets:

- Time-to-market – how long does it take the business to recognize a market opportunity and to translate this into a product or service and to bring it to the market?
- Time-to-serve – how long does it take to capture a customer's order and to deliver the product to the retail customer's satisfaction?
- Time-to-react — how long does it take to adjust the output of the business in response to volatile demand? Can the 'tap' be turned on or off quickly?

TIME-TO-MARKET

In these short life cycle markets, being able to spot trends quickly and to translate them into products in the shop in the shortest possible time has become a prerequisite for success. Companies that are slow to market can suffer in two ways. First, they miss a significant

91

sales opportunity that probably will not be repeated. Second, the supplier is likely to find that when the product finally arrives in the market place, demand is starting to fall away, leading to the likelihood of mark-downs. Figure 5.1 illustrates the double jeopardy confronting those organizations that are slow to market. New thinking in manufacturing strategy which has focused on flexibility and batch size reduction has clearly helped organizations in their search for quick response. The use of highly automated processes such as computer-aided manufacturing (CAM) has revolutionized the ability to make product changes as the season or the lifecycle progresses.

TIME-TO-SERVE

Traditionally in fashion industries orders from retailers have had to be placed on suppliers' books many months ahead of the season. Nine months was not unusual as a typical lead time. Clearly, in such an environment the risk of both obsolescence and stock-outs is high, as well as the significant inventory carrying cost that inevitably is

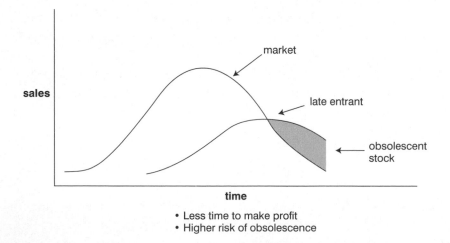

Figure 5.1 Shorter life cycles making timing crucial

incurred somewhere in the supply chain as a result of the lengthy pipeline.

Why should the order-to-delivery cycle be so long? It is not the time it takes to make or ship the product. More often the problem lies in the multiple steps that occur from the point at which a decision is taken to place an order, through the generation of the accompanying documentation (particularly in overseas transactions involving quota approvals, letters of credit, and so forth), into the suppliers' processes – which themselves are likely to be equally lengthy. Often the total time in manufacture is considerable because of the traditional, batch-based production methods. In other words, each step in the total manufacturing cycle is managed separately from each other and the quantities processed at each step are determined by so-called economic batch quantities. Furthermore, when manufacture takes place off-shore, considerable time is consumed in preparing documentation, in consolidating full container loads and in-bound customs clearance after lengthy surface transportation.

The underpinning philosophy that has led to this way of doing things is cost-minimization. Primarily, the costs that are minimized are costs of manufacture and, second, the costs of shipping. In fact, this view of cost is too narrow and ultimately self-defeating. The real issue is the total supply chain cost, the costs of obsolescence, forced mark-downs and inventory carrying costs.

TIME-TO-REACT

Ideally, in any market, an organization would want to be able to meet any customer requirement for the products on offer at the time and place the customer needs them. Clearly, some of the major barriers to this are those highlighted in the previous paragraphs ie time-to-market and time-to-serve. However, a further problem that organizations face as they seek to become more responsive to demand is that they are typically slow to recognize changes in real demand in the final market place. The challenge to any business in a fashion market is to be able to see 'real' demand. Real demand is what consumers are buying or requesting hour by hour, day by day. Because most supply chains are driven by orders (ie batched demand) which themselves are driven by forecasts and inventory replenishment, individual parties in the chain will have no real visibility of the final market place. As Figure 5.2 suggests, inventory hides demand. In other words, the fact that there will usually be multiple inventories from the retail shelf back through wholesalers to suppliers means that up-stream parties in the chain are unable to anticipate the changing needs of the customers other than through a forecast based as much upon judgment and guess-work as it is upon actual consumer demand.

THE LEAD-TIME GAP

The fundamental problem that faces many companies – not just those in fashion industries – is that the time it takes to source materials, convert them into products and move them into the market place is invariably longer than the time the customer is prepared to wait. This difference between what might be called the 'logistics pipeline' and the customers' order cycle time is termed the 'lead-time gap'. Conventionally, this gap was filled with a forecast-based inventory – there was no other way of attempting to ensure that there would be product available as and when customers demanded it.

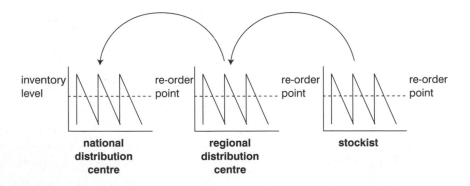

Figure 5.2 Inventory hides demand

The problem was that often it would be the 'wrong' inventory, for example, sizes, colours or styles that were not those actually demanded. Figure 5.3 highlights the problems of the lead-time gap which in the fashion industry is measured in months rather than weeks. The challenge to logistics management is to find ways to reduce, if not close, the gap.

CREATING LEAN SUPPLY CHAINS

Successful companies in fashion markets seem to be not just able to capture the imagination of the consumer with their products but are often characterized by their agility. In other words, by their ability to move quickly, uninhibited by cumbersome processes and lengthy supply chains. They are agile because they are 'lean'. How, then, is this leanness achieved? Many organizations are finding that it is possible to make significant improvements by adopting a twin strategy of simultaneously reducing the logistics lead time and capturing information sooner on actual customer demand.

One of the earliest and most celebrated exponents of this strategy is The Limited, a Columbus, Ohio-based apparel retailer. The company was one of the first in its industry to fully understand and exploit the economics of stock-turn and inventory management. Its flair for formula merchandising and skill in minimizing time-to-

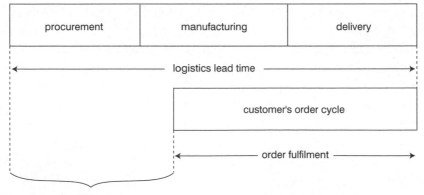

Figure 5.3 Lead-times

market changed the face of fashion retailing in the United States. Years before its competitors, The Limited developed computer-controlled global supply chains honed to detect and exploit new fashion trends with enviable speed and efficiency.

The Limited's teams of scouts continually comb the globe for hot new fashion ideas. Images of their finds are flashed back to the Columbus HQ, where they are promptly copied. Computer-aided design techniques are applied to bring the cut, colour and other details of the design into line with North American tastes. Moments later, small pilot orders are dispatched to EDI-linked suppliers in the low-cost manufacturing centres of Asia. Using Hong Kong as a consolidation centre, the goods are air freighted direct to The Limited's distribution centre in Columbus, in four times weekly shipments aboard a specially chartered 747 jumbo jet. The goods, ready labelled and price tagged for display, are sorted immediately, then, within two to three days, forwarded by road and air to retail sites all over the United States. The whole process takes approximately three to five weeks from order to in-store display and at the time it was introduced compared very favourably with the average nine months taken by its department store competitors.

While forecasting errors cannot be eliminated completely, The Limited developed systems to minimize the risks. First deliveries of new lines are forwarded to designated retail test sites. The sites are selected by sophisticated computer analysis which identifies the locations most likely to provide reliable predictive data on how well a given item will sell nationally. The systems can also pin-point the best days in the year to test new merchandise, as well as the optimum dates to order fabrics and start garment production. The test results are then used to determine the exact colour and size mix of subsequent orders, reducing further the possibility of acquiring the wrong stock.

Despite the precision planning, mistakes do inevitably occur, but The Limited's systems deal with these just as decisively. Every item arrives in the store with its anticipated 'in stock' and 'out of stock' date already defined, and between the two, predetermined windows of opportunity for reorder or order cancellation, as well as progressive markdown schedules for slow-moving stock. As a result, The Limited achieves five to six inventory turns a year, compared to the specialty store average of three or four (Aufreuter *et al.*, 1993)

CO-OPERATING TO COMPETE

In 1981 US-based garment suppliers had an 80 per cent share of the domestic market, but by 1987 the indigenous producers were struggling to hold on to a 60 per cent share of the combined apparel and textile markets. The US-based manufacturers were losing out badly to the Far Eastern suppliers of companies like The Limited and other low-margin niche retailers like The Gap. Tariffs undermined the initial cost advantage of sourcing off-shore, but as Leslie Wexner, chairman and founder of The Limited, explained in an interview with *Business Week* magazine, 'The problem with US textile suppliers is that they don't want to make what we want to buy' (Konrad, 1992: 33). The US mills didn't offer the same quality, styling or flexibility as their off-shore competitors. Economies of scale were the root of the problem. The US industry had the most modern production technology in the world, but most of it was geared to producing huge runs of basic cotton fabrics like denim and sheeting, the objective being to supply high volume consumers like jeans manufacturers and budget retailers such as Wal-Mart Stores Inc. as cost efficiently as possible. The fabric mills were unwilling to do special runs for small quantities of fashion fabrics.

Meanwhile, the textile manufacturers continued to search for competitive advantage on their own terms, forming the 'Crafted with Pride in the USA' Council Inc. The Council's 500 members funded a $100 million advertising programme to promote American-made clothing, through appeals to the patriotism of American consumers. However, they discovered that when it came to value-for-money clothing, US consumers were not that patriotic. It took some time, but eventually the Council realized that efficiency and consumer responsiveness were the industry's best defence.

The US manufacturers could not compete on labour costs, but distance was in their favour. It should be possible to compete in their own market by virtue of location, on time and transport costs. The Council commissioned consultants Kurt Salmon Associates to study US apparel industry supply chains. The results were alarming. The supply chains were too long and too badly co-ordinated to respond effectively to marketplace demands. Time-to-serve averaged one and a quarter years from textile loom to store rack. To reduce their own costs, stronger parties shifted the burden of inventory to weaker players, but the disconnected adversarial supply chains were still slow, costly and ineffective. Industry-wide, the cost of this inefficiency was estimated to be approximately $25 billion per year, around 20 per cent of the industry's total turnover (Stalk and Hout, 1990: 249). The supply chains could not absorb these costs, so they had been passed on to the customer – until the threat from imports became overwhelming.

The US industry had to find new ways of working if it was going to survive, so several pilot studies were commissioned to see if pipelines could be shortened through collaboration between retailers, apparel manufactures and textile producers. Among the first to participate in the pilot studies was Milliken & Co., the country's largest textile producer.

Milliken's performance before embarking on the experiment was as follows: Milliken received in-coming orders – slowly – by US mail. Weaving would normally be completed eight weeks after the yarn became available. Dyeing and finishing took a further four to five weeks. The stock would then be forwarded to the central warehouse until required by the customer. Throughput times were around 18–20 weeks from receipt of order. Keeping the factory operating at maximum capacity was the overriding priority.

After Milliken, an apparel manufacturer could take around 18–20 weeks from receipt of cloth to get the clothing to a retailer (Harvard Business School, 1993). The retailers, fearing stockouts, regularly over-ordered, increasing their carrying costs and resulting in mark-downs of excess stock. If the retailers' inventories got too high, then they would cut back on purchasing, leaving the manufacturers with excess stock. They in turn would cancel fabric orders, leaving Milliken holding unwanted inventory at its own cost.

In the pilot study, Milliken partnered with apparel manufacturer Seminole and Wal-Mart stores. Consultants monitored a single product line (basic slacks), measuring the sales and profit improvement delivered by the implementation of Quick Response. The results showed increased sales of 31 per cent and a 30 per cent improvement in inventory turns (Stalk and Hout, 1990). The exercise taught Milliken to look beyond its immediate customer – the apparel producer who paid the fabric invoice – so as to be responsive to the end consumers' requirements. If point-of-sale information could be shared between the partners, long-range forecasting, overstocking and order cancellations would no longer be necessary. Following the trail, Milliken began seeking out like-minded supply-chain partners who were willing to set aside short-term self-interest to create integrated supply chains.

QUICK RESPONSE AT BHS

In the United Kingdom also, integrated supply chains are emerging as larger retailers seek to establish closer collaborative relationships with their supply chain partners. Bhs is one of the country's largest high street retailers, with over 140 stores specializing in clothes for the modern woman and her family as well as decorative home furnishings, gifts and specialty packaged food. Since 1990, the company has been working to refine its replenishment systems to the point where the effective use of information has all but eliminated its need to hold inventory.

As long ago as the early 1980s, Bhs (then British Home Stores) recognized that the unfolding IT revolution could deliver significant improvements in logistics performance. Nevertheless it was to take several years – and the longest recession in retail history – before the benefits of harnessing IT to integrate the supply chain were realized.

Bhs had risen to the challenge of increased competition in the 1980s with the installation of an early EPOS system. It significantly improved the quality of sales data available to store managers. For the first time managers could identify sales trends almost as they emerged. This advance meant that the lengthy replenishment process could be activated without delay, allowing Bhs to maintain service levels in the face of increasing consumer demand. However, with the advent of recession, Bhs was one of many high street fashion retailers to experience a chilling of the retail climate. Customers suddenly became more discerning, more value-conscious, and much less prone to impulse buying, and profits plummeted.

In response, a new incoming Chairman and Chief Executive commissioned a wide-ranging added-value analysis of all aspects of Bhs' operations, including a major review of logistics, in November 1989. The review revealed that the benefits of improved replenishment had been at least partially negated by rising levels of obsolescent stock. The buoyant conditions of the early 1980s had allowed bad stock management practices to flourish. In the stores, slow-moving stock was marked down at the end of a season, but if it did not sell, then it was marked back up again and offered for sale the following year. Consequently, some stores regularly refused to accept incoming deliveries of new merchandise because their store rooms were overflowing with unsold stock, some of it up to four years old. The practice was wholly supported by inappropriate accounting assumptions which appeared to make stock more, rather than less, valuable with age.

The operational review was completed and in May 1990 Bhs announced that it had decided to concentrate on its core competencies of buying and selling, outsourcing all other aspects of its operations to specialist contractors. With their help Bhs went on to overhaul its stock management systems and embrace the principles of Quick Response. A radical rework of the retailers' supply chain followed, leading to the abandonment of over half of its 800 suppliers. Only those that were willing and able to adapt to the demanding requirements of a long-term retailer–supplier relationship were retained. In the stores, the EPOS system was upgraded, and improved co-ordination of the buying function led to a more coherent and harmonious product range. The costly bulging stock rooms rapidly gave way to a system where almost all stock is held by suppliers, the majority of whom are EDI linked to Bhs. By August 1991, an estimated 85 per cent of Bhs' merchandise was called through the replenishment system by EDI. Plans were in place to raise the figure to 100 per cent. The EDI links gave Bhs' suppliers access to data on how their own lines were selling in the stores, allowing them to detect emerging sales trends and anticipate replenishment orders. Goods could now be prepared and ready to ship by the time Bhs called them through the pipeline, reducing dramatically the time-to-react. The use of EDI all but eliminated order handling time, improving time-to-serve, as did the appointment of a single specialist contractor, Exel Logistics, to handle all Bhs' distribution.

Exel transports the merchandise – ready bar-coded for its final destination – from suppliers to a single dedicated warehouse at Atherstone, Warwickshire. Investment in the Atherstone site provided Bhs with a single, fully integrated, distribution system capable of handling both cartons and hanging garments – the first of its kind in Europe. There the merchandise is sorted and dispatched within 24 hours to Bhs' UK stores. The daily deliveries arrive at the shops at between 06.00 and 10.00 each morning, just in time to meet the lunch time shopping rush.

In five years Bhs' replenishment cycles have been reduced to the point where 60 per cent of all orders arrive the next day and the full 100 per cent are released within 48 hours. The daily deliveries have reduced storage space requirements on Bhs retail sites from 20 per cent to 10 per cent over the last 10 years, with further reductions anticipated for new retail locations.

The Bhs example demonstrates further the commanding position of large retailers within their respective supply chains. Not surprisingly it is still the apparel manufacturer and most likely their suppliers that hold the lion's share of what inventory remains within the logistics pipeline. Nevertheless, those suppliers who remain are by virtue of the EDI system less exposed to the risk of obsolescent stock. They are also much more likely to receive a greater share of business from Bhs, though this too is not without its risks.

IMPORTANCE OF SUPPLY CHAIN INTEGRATION

Of course, there are a handful of fashion retailers with their own integrated design, manufacturing and distribution operations who have – or rather should have – almost complete control of their supply chains. Laura Ashley was one such retailer which, despite numerous changes of management and business strategy, has consistently failed to get to grips with the management of its own inventory. The history of the company, from its flotation in 1985 to the announcement of otherwise encouraging results in early 1997, is a lamentable catalogue of logistics opportunities lost (Peck and Christopher, 1994; Skeel, 1997).

In contrast, the Spanish-based apparel company Zara provides an encouraging example of how an integrated design, manufacturing and retail group is successfully managing its international supply chains. The first Zara shop opened in La Coruña, Northern Spain in 1975. In just over 20 years the business had grown to become one of Spain's leading textile and apparel companies, with sizeable production facilities in Spain, purchasing operations in Southeast Asia and the Caribbean, a finance holding company in The Netherlands and around 200 retail outlets (owned by the company) in Europe and the Americas (Bonache and Cerviño, 1995; Bonache and Cerviño, 1996).

Like Italian fashion giant Benetton, Zara produces a single global product range, designed to appeal to an international target market, in this case fashion-conscious 18 to 35 year-olds (the same market segment as targeted by The Limited and The Gap in the United States, Next in the United Kingdom and C&A in Germany).

The whole process of supplying goods to the stores begins with the cross-functional teams, comprising fashion, commercial and retail specialists, working within Zara's design department at the company's headquarters in La Coruña. The designs reflect the latest in international fashion trends, with inspiration gleaned from visits to fashion shows, competitors' stores, university campuses, pubs, cafes and clubs, plus any other venues or events deemed to be relevant to the lifestyles of the target customers. The team's knowledge of fashion trends is supplemented further by regular inflows of EPOS data and other information from all of the company's stores and sites around the world.

Fashion specialists within the design department are responsible for the initial designs, fabric selection and choice of prints and colours. It is then up to the team's commercial management specialists to ascertain the likely commercial viability of the items proposed. If the design is accepted, the commercial specialists proceed to negotiate with suppliers, agree purchase prices, analyse costs, margins and fix a standard cross-currency price position for the garment. The size of the production run – ie the number of garments required – and launch dates (the latter vary between countries in accordance with custom and climate) are also determined at this point.

Raw materials are procured through the company's buying offices in the United Kingdom, China and The Netherlands, with most of the materials themselves coming in from Mauritius, New Zealand, Australia, Morocco, China, India, Turkey, Korea, Italy and Germany. This global sourcing policy using a broad supplier base provides the widest possible selection of fashion fabrics, while reducing the risk of dependence on any source or supplier. Approximately 40 per cent of garments – those with the broadest and least transient appeal – are imported as finished goods from low-cost manufacturing centres in the Far East. The rest are produced in Spain, using Zara's own highly automated factories and a network of smaller contractors. Two guiding principles underlie all of its operations: quick response to market needs and working without inventory. Here lies the company's principal source of competitive advantage.

Zara's manufacturing systems are in many ways similar to those developed and employed so successfully by Benetton in Northern

Italy, but refined using ideas developed in conjunction with Toyota. Only those operations which enhance cost efficiency through economies of scale are conducted in-house (such as dyeing, cutting, labelling and packaging). All other manufacturing activities, including the labour-intensive finishing stages, are completed by networks of more than 300 small subcontractors, each specializing in one particular part of the production process or garment type. These subcontractors work exclusively for Zara's parent, Inditex SA. In return, they receive the necessary technological, financial and logistical support required to achieve stringent time and quality targets. Inventory costs are kept to a minimum because Zara pays only for the completed garments. The system is flexible enough to cope with sudden changes in demand, though production is always kept at a level slightly below expected sales, to keep stock moving. Zara has opted for undersupply, viewing it as a lesser evil than holding slow-moving or obsolete stock.

Finished goods are forwarded to the company's huge distribution centre in La Coruña, where they are labelled, price-tagged (all items carry international price tags showing the price in all relevant currencies) and packed. From there they travel by third-party contractors by road and/or air to their penultimate destinations. The shops themselves receive deliveries of new stock on a twice-weekly basis, according to shop-by-shop stock allocations calculated by the design department. The whole production cycle takes only two weeks. In an industry where lead-times of many months are still the norm, Zara has reduced its lead-time gap for more than half of the garments it sells to a level unmatched by any of its European or North American competitors.

Whether lead-times for mass-produced high fashion items can be reduced further remains to be seen, but the technology of Quick Response is providing other garment manufactures with new value-adding service opportunities to boost sales of some perennial fashion favourites.

Levi Strauss & Co have been making hard-wearing classic blue jeans for almost one and a half centuries. Until very recently the quality of the products and the strength of the brand were enough to guarantee a market for Levi's jeans. But intensified competition and ever more demanding retailers have latterly pushed the issue of customer service high up the management agenda.

From the early 1990s Levi Strauss has invested in more responsive and efficient manufacturing and supply systems. In its US factories, lead-times and inventory have been reduced significantly by replacing relatively inflexible assembly lines with self-managing teams, using leading-edge manufacturing and communications technology. Meanwhile Levi's retailer inventory management system 'LeviLink' has improved product availability, replenishment, and overall standards of service to the point where after a century of mass production Levi Strauss can again offer its customers individually made-to-measure jeans.

Levi's 'Perfect Pair' service provides female customers with custom-made tapered-leg jeans, for only a few pounds more than off-the-peg alternatives. The company already offered its mass-produced standard jeans in over 170 women's, junior and petite sizes and fits, but the introduction of Perfect Pair aimed to cater for its most discerning denim buyers. The service was launched in the United States, Canada and then the United Kingdom through Levi's own Original Levi Stores. The in-store fitting process lasts approximately 20 minutes. Trained female sales assistants take the customer's measurements, which are then fed into a computer terminal. Using specially designed software, the system identifies a code number for an appropriate pair of in-store trial jeans. The customer tries them on, so that minor deviations in size and shape can be recorded. When the customer is totally satisfied with the fit, details of the order are forwarded by modem to a Levi's factory in Tennessee. There a dedicated team make up the Perfect Pair, for delivery within three weeks. The customer's details are retained on computer by Levi, and a bar code displaying the customer reference number is sewn into the waistband of each Perfect Pair. The customer can then contact the company at any time to order additional pairs of jeans, by simply quoting her barcode number.

The introduction of the 'Perfect Pair' was heralded by industry analysts as a major breakthrough in customer service, and sent sales soaring by up to 300 per cent at early test sites. Although made-to-measure products still account for only a tiny percentage of Levi Strauss's sales, industry observers believe that bespoke products are about to become an everyday feature of the electronic shopping malls.

These examples show how significant improvements in performance can be made by adopting a twin strategy of simultaneously reducing the logistics lead time and capturing information sooner on actual customer demand. The prerequisites for achieving these dual goals are:

- understand the process;
- eliminate non-value-adding activities;
- improve end-to-end pipeline visibility.

UNDERSTAND THE PROCESS

Fundamental to the development of more responsive supply chains is the detailed understanding of how and where time is consumed at every step, from the sourcing of materials through manufacturing and the distribution channel to the final market. Supply chain mapping is a powerful means of highlighting the lengthy processes and the numerous stock holding points that characterize so many industries. Essentially, mapping seeks to flow-chart each activity in the chain from order entry through to final delivery to gain an insight into why the supply chain is as lengthy as it is.

Examination of the output of a supply chain mapping exercise will often reveal that a significant proportion of the total pipeline time is consumed in non-value-adding activities. A non-value-adding activity is one that does not add to the total value of the product to the customer or the consumer. So time spent as intermediate product, in lengthy re-ordering processes or as finished inventory, for example, is not creating additional value for the customer – only additional cost.

ELIMINATE NON-VALUE-ADDING ACTIVITIES

It follows that the real key to time compression in the logistics pipeline is through the elimination or reduction of time spent on non-value-adding activities. Hence, contrary to a common misconception, time compression is not based on the idea of performing activities faster but rather performing fewer of them. The old cliché 'work smarter not harder' is particularly relevant in this context.

As Hammer and Champy have pointed out, many of the processes used in our organizations were designed for a different era. They tend to be paper-based, with many – often redundant – manual steps. They are sequential and batch-oriented rather than parallel and capable of changing quickly from one task to another. Even though eliminating or reducing such activities may actually increase cost, the end result will often be more cost-effective. For example, shipping direct from factories to end customers may be more expensive in terms of the unit cost of transport compared to shipping via a regional distribution centre, because time spent as inventory in the distribution centre is usually non-value-adding time (as well as the time spent in receiving and handling into the store and out).

The challenge therefore is to convince management that a wider view of supply chain costs needs to be adopted – not some narrow cost concept based on manufacturing costs or shipping costs alone. More particularly, the impact of eliminating non-value-adding activities on marketplace responsiveness needs to be given a much greater weight when the fundamental processes of the business are being reviewed.

IMPROVE END-TO-END PIPELINE VISIBILITY

We have already highlighted the problems generated by conventional inventory-based logistics systems – a key concern being the lack of 'visibility' of demand. In other words, in lengthy, and increasingly global, pipelines, managers in one part of the chain are

LOGISTICS AND RETAIL MANAGEMENT

not aware of the upstream or downstream situation regarding levels of demand or supply or current inventory levels. As a result, each step in the chain is forced to forecast requirements and to build an inventory buffer in an attempt to manage the inherent uncertainty in such systems. However, the creation of these inventory buffers only serves to exacerbate the situation.

How can this problem of visibility be resolved and how can we move away from forecast-driven logistics towards demand-driven logistics? Essentially, the requirement is to capture information on consumer demand in as close to real time as possible and to share that information with all the upstream players in the total supply chain. By gaining early warning of demand it clearly becomes more possible for upstream suppliers to be able to respond to that demand.

The breakthroughs in information technology and its application in logistics have enabled 'quick response' replenishment to become a reality. The increasingly widespread application of the 'Efficient Consumer Response' (ECR) concept in retailing has shown how it is possible to achieve significant improvements in meeting volatile demand but with dramatically less inventory.

To make this type of demand-driven logistics a reality requires a totally different model of buyer–supplier relationships in the supply chain. The underpinning philosophy has to be that shared information enables all parties in the chain to benefit through reduced inventories, better use of capacity, fewer stock-outs and less obsolescence.

CONCLUSION

Fashion markets, by their very nature, demand highly responsive logistics support. The paradox is that, over the years, many of the supply chains for fashion products have actually *lengthened* as manufacturers and retailers have sought to reduce costs by seeking to source product from low labour cost markets, often thousands of miles from the end consumer. The lessons that can be learned from those companies that have recognized that timely response and agility are the prerequisites for success are significant. In particular, the key message seems to be that without an integrated supply chain, driven by demand data captured at the point of sale and shared across the chain, even the most appealing designs will not be enough to ensure success in fashion markets.

REFERENCES

Aufreuter, N, Karch, N and S and Smith, C (1993) The engine of success in retailing, *McKinsey Quarterly*, 3, pp 101–16

Bonache, J and Cerviño, J (1995) *Empirical Evidence of Achieving Local Sensibility, Global Interaction and Organizational Learning Without the Use of Expatriates*, case study, Universidad Carlos III, Madrid

Bonache, J and Cerviño, J (1996) Zara–El Tejido Internacional, in *Multinacionales Españolas: Algunos casos relevantes*, ed J.J. Duràn Herrera, Coleccíon Economía y Gestión Internacional, Editorial Pirámide, Madrid

Fitzpatrick, R (1994) Another country, *Retail Week*, 25 March 1994, p. 18

Hammer, M and Champy, J (1993) *Re-engineering the Corporation*, HarperCollins, New York

Harvard Business School (1993) Time based competition, *Harvard Business School Management Programmes* (video), programme 2

Konrad, W (1992) Why Leslie Wexner shops overseas, *Business Week*, 3 February, p 33

Peck, H and Christopher, M (1994) Laura Ashley: the logistics challenge, in *Cases in Retail Management*, ed P McGoldrick, pp 310–27, Pitman, London

Skeel, S (1997) Laura Ashley targets let Iverson pocket £1m pay, *Daily Mail*, 3 May 1997

Stalk, G Jr. and Hout, TM (1990) *Competing Against Time*, Free Press, New York, p 249

6

RETHINKING EFFICIENT REPLENISHMENT IN THE GROCERY SECTOR

Phil Whiteoak

ECR – A FAD OR THE FUTURE?

The idea of Efficient Consumer Response (ECR) is sweeping through the board rooms of most fast-moving consumer goods manufacturers and retailers in the advanced economies of the world. The vision of ECR Europe, 'Working together to fulfil consumer wishes better, faster and at less cost', is driving a unique initiative by suppliers, distributors and retailers that claims to provide European consumers with the best possible value, service and variety of products through a collaborative approach to improving the supply chain. Debate still rages as to whether ECR is, at best, a philosophy which can genuinely improve consumer value or, at worst, simply a new management fad. Alternatively, it may be seen as a tactic for gaining control in a trading relationship or simply as a toolkit for tinkering with the complex balances of the supply chain. Indeed, in a provocative address to the 39th CIES Annual Executive Congress in Paris in June 1996, Professor Lou Stern of Northwestern University, USA, remarked, 'ECR is a short-term survival tactic, a mandatory set of tactics which may allow the business to buy time . . . it does not ask the question "How do people really want to shop for food?" Rather, it assumes that the answer is the existing supermarket . . . and goes on from there to address value chain logistics.' He also decried the notion of collaboration: 'partnership as it's practised today is manipulation . . . we'll be partners if it benefits me.'

There is no doubt that today's grocery markets are intensively competitive. The internationalization of trade and the rapid pace of technological development are creating major challenges, even for well-established businesses. Globally, increasingly sophisticated consumers are driving both manufacturers and retailers into developing extended product ranges and into trading in more countries and distribution channels. These trends tend to dilute traditional economies of scale. Supply chains are becoming longer and more complex as a result of the need for sourcing the materials to support these markets. Environmental legislation, the pressure of reducing cycle times and a focus on customer service are constraining the drive for efficiency and cost reduction. Addressing value chain logistics is thus not to be disparaged and offers the logistics community a worthwhile opportunity to improve its performance within this dynamic environment, notwithstanding other breakthroughs in fulfilling consumer needs, such as home tele-shopping. In any event, there will always remain the need to move goods efficiently from the point of production to the point of consumption. In short, there will always be a 'supply chain'. In grocery, the opportunity is indeed worthwhile: the retail value of European grocery markets is in excess of 700 billion ecu, with supply chain costs estimated to be around 10 per cent per cent of sales. Small improvements in logistics efficiency across this market can thus generate huge cash savings. The building of a critical mass of businesses that share the vision and that co-operate and exchange information to employ a number of 'improvement concepts' is the key to unlocking this benefit.

The improvement concepts within the ECR initiative embrace Category Management (which aims to optimize the range of products stocked in store, the efficiency of promotions and new product introductions), Product Replenishment and Enabling Technologies. Broadly, these address 'demand side' and 'supply side' activities and the information systems necessary to support them, and consist more or less of a catalogue of techniques and a guide for their application. No single technique is universally effective and, while the application of any one technique may generate benefits for one supply chain player, it may have adverse consequences for the other. This chapter reviews the facts and myths behind current 'efficient replenishment' thinking and proposes a supplementary approach to the current practice.

EFFICIENT REPLENISHMENT

Both in the United States and in Europe the initial focus of the ECR movement was product replenishment, or, as it has come to be known, Efficient Replenishment. The reasons for this are simple: first, the size of the prize to be won in streamlining grocery supply chains is huge – in the United States it was first estimated that the total grocery supply chain inventory could be reduced from more than 100 days of sales to around 60 days by the application of ER techniques. Although in European supply chains the stock is on average already substantially below the American aspiration, their annual operating costs of 70 billion ecu offer tempting opportunities. Second, so far, the subject of ER has been relatively non-contentious. Hitherto, it has not figured greatly in trading debates between retailers and their suppliers about range, promotions and profitability and has frequently been left to the logistics functions of either business to resolve.

However, there is now a growing awareness across Europe that ER is a strategic tool for improving margins and reducing cash tied up in working capital. The danger is that the pursuit of these benefits by any one party without consideration of the possible impacts on other players in the supply chain can significantly disturb the balance of costs between manufacturers and retailers. Despite setting out to create a climate of collaboration in which all parties should benefit, the ECR movement may add to this risk of destabilization by promoting a particular technique without adequate explanation of the most appropriate criteria for its application. This idea is explored below.

What is efficient replenishment? Figure 6.1 illustrates the concept as a smooth, continual flow of product, matched to consumption and supported by a timely, accurate and paperless information flow.

The techniques often described for delivering this vision are illustrated in Figure 6.2. Of these, Continuous Replenishment and Cross-Docking are probably amongst the most frequently discussed, and perhaps the least well understood.

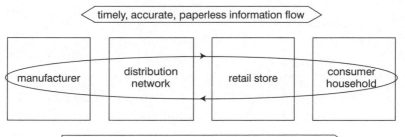

Figure 6.1 Concept of Efficient Replenishment

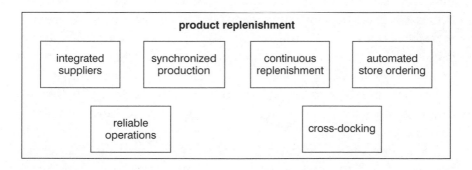

Figure 6.2 Techniques for Efficient Replenishment

CONTINUOUS REPLENISHMENT PROGRAMMES (CRP)

CRP comes in many forms. The most commonly described is Vendor Managed Inventory (VMI) in a Fixed Order Quantity (FOQ) environment. This requires *daily* review of the retail sales and stock position, with an order only suggested when necessary to meet previously agreed target stocking levels. The replenishment algorithm uses actual retail sales information for forecasting future sales, on the basis of which a new order is calculated. In order to work effectively, this must have Electronic Data Interchange (EDI) communication from the retailer to the supplier and probably needs intervention or examination by the supplier's customer service department every day.

What is the objective of this sort of CRP? By gaining *control* of retail replenishment processes a manufacturer aims to manage ordering behaviour towards more efficient load building. The manufacturer is also responsible for managing product availability at the point to which goods are delivered (which presupposes the manufacturer can do this better than the retailer), hence assuring support for his promotional and feature activity and thereby moving towards preferred supplier status. The manufacturer does gain the benefit of market intelligence about sell-through, but overall the information is of little further value unless it can be obtained from a sufficiently large population of customers to enable its use in the modification of sales forecasts and production plans. In any case, this is likely to be most suitable for retail outlets where there are store back-room stocks and where orders are still raised directly on the supplier. It is also suitable for retail regional distribution centres (RDCs) which are responsible for their own replenishment and which are prepared to relinquish control to the supplier. It is most likely to be suitable for lines with large volume sales and forecastable promotional impact.

A variant on this is called Co-managed inventory (CMI) where retailers share information about promotional programmes of all suppliers in the category with vendors participating in the scheme.

There may well be legal limitations on this under European competition law. In the United Kingdom, there are few applications of this sort of VMI with the major multiple retailers.

VMI may also run in a Fixed Order Cycle (FOC) environment. Typically, this is used to service smaller outlets which are not capable of managing their own inventories well and where it is only cost-effective for a supplier to make a sales call or a delivery weekly or fortnightly at most. In this situation, either the supplier's representative or merchandiser counts stock or, prompted by a small discount as an incentive, the customer counts it and returns a balance for each stocked product by telephone or fax to the supplier's office where it is keyed into the VMI system. The movement between the current and previous stock balance is used to calculate the retail sales. Otherwise the mathematics are the same as before. This approach is suitable for use where customers are not sufficiently well-advanced to be able to support EDI connections. The prime aim of this style of application is to be a sales support tool for gaining control of in-store availability to support display and feature selling. Real examples of this exist in the independent wholesale sector. The key elements in the replenishment here are the order review cycle, the replenishment lead time and the target safety stock level.

Both FOQ and FOC VMI systems could also be run by suppliers upstream of grocery product manufacturers to keep factories supplied on a similar basis. There are also some radical approaches now in existence where suppliers are expected to keep factory input buffers full or topped-up with no formal communication of expected requirements.

In the case of the large multiple retailers in the United Kingdom, their aim is very much to run a CRP process in which they retain control of the replenishment (in order only to have to deal with a single uniform process) and move towards a daily call off on very short lead times. This is undoubtedly continuous replenishment but not VMI. However, there are initiatives running in the United Kingdom on joint promotional planning and, although these may be part of a CRP initiative, they are not what is commonly understood to be CRP in the industry.

Very generally, in retailer CRP programmes a number of functions are required: aggregation of store demand (via Automated Store Ordering) to a total demand on an RDC, calculation of the RDC replenishment requirement, conversion of the RDC replenishment need into a supply instruction (sales order process/despatch preparation). These processes need to be carried out regardless of whether they are done by the customer or the supplier. In some applications in the United States, retailers have delegated the responsibility for both store and RDC replenishment to vendors, giving them access to store scanning data. The reason for transferring responsibility for, for example, RDC replenishment from retailer to manufacturer is either about gaining control or demonstrating a mutual advantage. In many cases supply chain partners may not be willing to relinquish control, irrespective of the quality of the case argued.

CROSS-DOCKING

Cross-docking is a technique in which goods arriving at an RDC are unloaded from the inbound vehicle and moved from the goods receiving area 'across the dock' for marshalling with other goods for onward despatch without being put away into stock. This technique has long been a necessity for very short-life, perishable products. There are broadly two types: full pallet and case level cross-docking. The former is often used in large geographic areas (such as the United States) where a full vehicle of full pallets moves from the production source to a regional cross-dock point. The full pallets are then off-loaded and moved across the dock for consolidation with full pallets from another source to enable the building of a full vehicle load for onward transfer to the final destination, which is likely to be a warehouse local to a number of stores where the full pallets are put away into stock for subsequent let-down, picking and delivery to store. Typically, the picking at this stage is the traditional 'pick-by-store' technique.

Case level cross-docking embraces a new concept – pick-by-line to zero. The key elements here are timely delivery and just the right quantity. In this case, there is usually only one move between the manufacturer and the store. At the RDC, lanes are set out containing roll-cages to be delivered to each store served by the RDC. As the goods arrive, they are broken down and the appropriate quantity of each product line is loaded into the roll cages for each store. Full pallets of single products are no longer necessarily appropriate – only the quantity of product required by the stores need be delivered in order to avoid having to put a surplus away into stock. A strategy of pick-by-line cross-docking has obvious appeal to retailers. Not only is working capital freed-up from inventory holding, but also the assets and people required for managing warehouse stocks (put-away, let-down, etc.) are no longer required. These represent approximately 30 per cent of the operating costs of a conventional stock-holding retail RDC. Most importantly, though, the freeing-up of buildings previously occupied by racking and stock creates space. This space in turn enables throughput capacity to be created. Thus, from a simple change in supplier delivery behaviour, a retailer can generate significant increases in his capacity to process volume growth in the business without major investment in buildings, plant and equipment.

From a manufacturer's perspective, the implications of such a change are that they have to be able to supply on short lead times, to support daily review of order requirements, to make deliveries scheduled to meet retailer receiving requirements and, above all, to maintain consistently reliable service levels.

SYNCHRONIZED PRODUCTION

This technique aims to match manufacturing production cycles with retail sales and in many batch-oriented packeted grocery production processes remains a pipe dream. Canning, bottling and carton-filling lines are expensive to install and are often used to produce many different finished products. Inherently, they are designed to run in cycles and therefore to 'make for stock'. Often, too, their upstream supply chains are extended, with material availability constrained by crop yields. To move closer to 'making to order' requires clear communication and effective implementation of customer marketing plans to achieve predictable consumer offtake. Retail buying behaviour must be synchronizsed with offtake levels and there needs to be adequate instantaneous logistics capacity to accommodate the peaks and troughs in demand. This all needs to be allied to shorter manufacturing cycles and run lengths and faster changeovers to support the burgeoning number of product lines necessary to keep pace with increasingly demanding consumers. As order-to-delivery lead times continue to be squeezed by retailers at a rate not matched by corresponding improvements in manufacturing cycle and response times, the possibility of 'making-to-order' remains unattainable. The reality in most packeted grocery plants remains that of 'making-for-stock'. This requires an accurate sales forecast to be made, which, in an environment of increasing promotional activity, continues to be a prerequisite of efficient replenishment.

Notwithstanding these difficulties, it should go without saying that Reliable Operations (that is, the ability to produce the planned product at the right time, at the right quality and in the right quantity) are fundamental to being able to fulfil retail demand reliably and at the minimum level of stock. Integrated Suppliers are part of a concept in which the suppliers of manufacturers are part of the same 'virtual enterprise' as the manufacturer. Often they are responsible for keeping factories supplied with materials on a continuous replenishment basis along exactly similar lines to those outlined above for CRP activity between manufacturers and retailers. The idea of integration as a supply chain development tactic is discussed in more detail later.

SUPPLY CHAIN TYPES

An alternative way of assessing the use of these techniques is to consider the different types of grocery supply chains in which they might be used. Figure 6.3 sets out the four main types which characterize 80 per cent of European grocery supply.

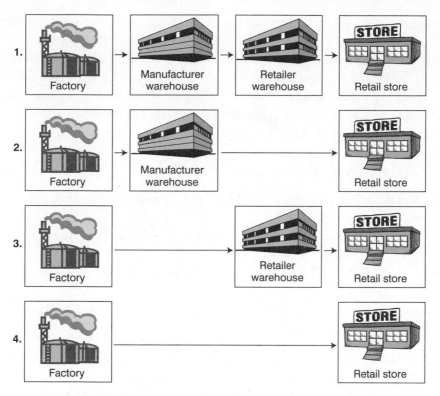

Figure 6.3 Main types of grocery supply chain

These generally have the following characteristics:

1. Make to stock production with RDC delivery.
2. Make to stock production with direct store delivery.
3. Make to order production with RDC delivery.
4. Make to order production with direct store delivery.

The first is the routine method of distribution in the greater part of European grocery markets, typically applicable to large volumes of ambient temperature chain goods, produced in cyclical batch processes, and where retail stores have little or no back-room stock. The second is typically used in less advanced markets, where stores retain stock back-rooms or in markets where large deliveries can be made to very large hypermarkets. The third applies in perishable goods chains where volumes are insufficient for efficient delivery direct to store and a consolidation is necessary in the retail RDC to drive up vehicle utilization. The last also applies in perishable chains, typically where large volume, very short life items are sourced locally for stores (eg milk, bread). Exceptionally, this route may be used for 'specials' such as display pallets direct from factory to store.

The key replenishment processes are

- Retail store with automated (computer assisted) store ordering (CAO);
- Retail RDC with Purchase Order Management (POM) based on aggregated store orders;
- Retail RDC with Continuous Replenishment Programmes (CRP) by supplier;
- Supplier warehouse/ or supplier factory with order processing/ despatch preparation.

Note that even if suppliers undertake CRP, there will remain a need for order processing to convert requests for a delivery into a vehicle despatch and to apply pricing. The only processes which potentially overlap or are duplicated are RDC POM and supplier CRP.

Note also the role of the retail RDC. This may be to hold stock, but is primarily to consolidate store deliveries across a range of suppliers. In the event that the RDC is stockless, then its supply is more likely to be closely coupled with the store CAO, suggesting that vendor-managed CRP is less likely to be attractive to retailers. Retailers will wish to remain in control of store replenishment. Thus CRP programmes are not likely to represent the long-term trade direction.

In summary, retail distribution of ambient goods will in the main be focused through RDCs, not principally via direct store delivery. These RDCs will continue to destock via lead time reductions and increased order frequency. Suppliers will see the effects of this in smaller, more frequent orders, more order picking and reduced vehicle utilization.

Principles already successfully applied to fresh food and private label distribution will be applied to ambient and frozen branded goods. Stock will only be held in store and will be eliminated in retail RDCs by daily ordering and same-day delivery seven days per week driven by checkout scanning data and significant investment in replenishment systems and technology. Order quantities will no longer be governed by achieving best terms conditions but rather will aim to provide 'just the right quantity'. Stock at RDCs will be eliminated as products are 'picked by line' on arrival, moved 'across the dock' and assembled for store delivery. Deliveries to RDCs will therefore be scheduled to optimize RDC resource utilization and to consolidate store delivery transport into fewer vehicles. Ultimately, deliveries arriving at RDCs will be required to have been pre-assembled into roll-cages. Quality of manufacturer service (in terms of delivery accuracy and timing) will be the key to maintaining product availability in store. This will lead to peaking of picking and vehicle loading activity in manufacturer warehouses (ie more instantaneous spare distribution capacity will be required), 'real-time' processing of orders, automatic allocations of stock and more responsive supply systems. Electronic Data Interchange (EDI) will be a prerequisite to enable the achievement of the necessary fast cycle times of the replenishment process. Bar-coded product identification and case marking will be essential to facilitate the automation of goods handling and the elimination of errors. Visibility of stock available to commit becomes essential. There will be no time to replan or redeploy. The role of the manufacturer's customer service clerk will therefore be much reduced because there will no longer be the opportunity to participate directly in the order management process.

A fundamental strategy for countering such trends will be the use of genuine cost-related price cards which identify and pass on the costs of such added-value servicing arrangements and which promote the type of ordering behaviour better suited to the nature of the manufacturer's production process. This will enable manufacturers to limit the erosion of their lead times so that the peaking of the requirements for distribution capacity can be smoothed.

However, requests to expose manufacturer logistics costs will increasingly become a component of the trading debate. Activity-based costing in the logistics network will thus be the key to price card determination and for providing the information for these discussions.

In parallel there will be a retail focus on the efficiency of vehicle utilization, featuring requests for customer collection, use of consolidators for smaller volume business and pooling with third parties in intermediate warehouses. This will lead to demands for ex-works pricing, cherry-picking of routes by retailers and loss of control of vehicles by suppliers. However, there will be a potential for the creative use of shared fleets to increase vehicle utilization. These practices will be applied to routine replenishment. Exceptionally, different practices and routes to store may be used for special or promotional lines.

Finally, downstream of the supplier warehouse, and from a supplier viewpoint, replenishment consists of two parallel processes. The *physical response* (ie moving goods through the supply chain) and *planning* the availability of the appropriate stock. The ECR work to date has tended to focus on the inventory replenishment and ordering processes between manufacturer–retailer pairs and, other than cross-docking, little attention has been paid until now to improving the physical aspects of moving the goods.

IMPACT OF LEAD TIME REDUCTIONS ON MANUFACTURER INVENTORY LEVELS

The foregoing discussion identifies areas where manufacturers will need to increase their response capability within the physical distribution network. Will these changes also impact their stock holding? Since, in the main, large producers of packaged goods manufacture in cycles, they will have to continue to manufacture for stock, but the uncontrolled erosion of lead time described above will reduce their opportunity for 'make-to-order' production and increase their dependence on sales forecasts to plan cycle stocks to meet the service requirements. Changes in retail physical distribution practice could transfer inventory holding and handling activity upstream to manufacturers and potentially have an adverse impact on the capacity and efficiency of supplier distribution warehouses and transport utilization. Business processes and systems will therefore need to be developed to support parallel activities in fast-cycle operational distribution and the planning and scheduling of the necessary inventory and logistics resources.

However, this analysis relates mainly to developments in large-scale retail grocery. Clearly, the situation in other channels is varied and dynamically changing. The logistics networks manufacturers provide must be able to adapt to the needs of these other channels as well as providing the capacity to respond to the grocery trends.

Most packeted goods manufacturers are primarily 'make-for-stock' organizations. Generally, customer order-to-delivery lead times are already less than production cycle times and, broadly, further reductions in delivery lead time will not materially affect cycle stocks. However, as lead times are reduced, the 'actual' component of immediate future sales (the order bank) is also reduced, increasing the forecast component. Therefore, the element of safety stock which covers forecast accuracy is likely to increase.

Manufacturer programmes for stock reduction must therefore hinge on reducing cycle times and improving forecast accuracy. Cycle times are determined by the following:

- economic run lengths (a trade-off of material batch efficiencies with changeover and downtime costs, together with achievable line output rates thus determines the amount to be made in one run); rate of sale (determining how often this amount should be made);
- available line capacity.

Militating against shorter run lengths are loss of capacity through downtime, increased costs due to changeovers and reduced efficiency. However, increasing range complexity within a fixed plant configuration will *demand* shorter run lengths and thus more frequent cycles.

A branded product manufacturer has to supply many different channels and individual retailers. The manufacturer must therefore balance capacity across a multiplicity of customers and thus efficient consumer response with an individual customer cannot extend into the daily scheduling of production.

THE BRANDED MANUFACTURER'S RESPONSE

Manufacturers are already beginning to provide support for these fast cycle requirements by increasing the capacity and efficiency of their distribution networks and by providing new order management systems. However, these only provide the capability to deliver more efficiently whatever stock is available. Manufacturers therefore also need to provide support for improved planning processes to assure supply availability to meet customer service performance targets and to establish lowest target stock levels to achieve this service level. This has to be achieved whilst making the appropriate trade-offs with manufacturing and supply chain operating costs.

This suggests a number of information strategies as shown in Table 6.1.

SUPPLY CHAIN INTEGRATION

Supply chain integration between trading partners is often cited as an essential technique to achieve improvements in the efficiency of the replenishment processes. It is important to understand what is meant by the concept – integration can be a technique for aiding optimization of the supply chain but it can also be a means whereby one participant in the chain gains control over a greater part of the chain. So far, the integration activity reported in the ECR literature has been mainly focused on execution level processes, typically operating between manufacturer and retailer pairs, or *along* the chain. For example, the principal techniques described are CRP and cross-docking. Few examples have been seen of *across* the chain

Table 6.1 Information strategies to support improved planning processes

Objective	Strategy
to improve in-market forecasting	customer-level activity management and joint forecasting initiatives based on point of sale data; category management techniques such as shelf space planning
to improve efficiency of transport	develop new approaches to shared transport management
to improve factory scheduling	implementation of Master Production Scheduling (MPS) and Manufacturing Resource Planning (MRP) programmes (these address having the right stock in total although not necessarily in the right place)
to improve in-market stock deployment	implementation of Distribution Requirements Planning (DRP) systems; use of vendor-managed CRP programmes
to improve financial processes	use of Electronic Funds Transfer techniques
to improve administrative efficiency	development of new EDI transactions (eg confirmation of proof of delivery); use EDI price or promotion databases; adoption of 'green lane' delivery arrangements (no checking of supplier deliveries at retail RDCs)

integration and there has certainly been little evidence of integrated planning. Now, given that one manufacturer supplies many customers and one customer is supplied by many manufacturers, the idea of considering the replenishment process in this context as a chain is erroneous. Supply chains are in fact supply *networks* in which complexity is increasing rapidly.

So far, improvements in efficiency have come from the application of techniques, none of which is universally beneficial. Integration *along* a chain is a technique to enable one partner to gain *control*; integration *across* the network will help overall *optimization*. Some consequences of 'along the chain' integration are considered below.

CONSEQUENCES OF ALONG THE CHAIN INTEGRATION

Figure 6.4 below illustrates the evolution of UK retail grocery distribution practice. The x-axis of the graph considers the period of time since the 1970s. The y-axis uses as its measure of efficiency the rate of retail inventory turn.

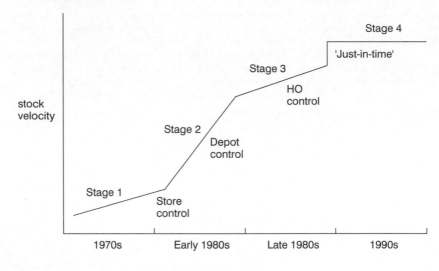

Figure 6.4 Evolution of UK grocery distribution

Over the last 20 years or so there have been four stages in this evolutionary process. The first, 'Store Control', typical during the 1970s, is characterized by direct delivery from manufacturers to stores, with store inventory levels controlled by the branch manager, often 'assisted' by the manufacturer's representative. Usually, one order was placed each week on a week's delivery lead time, with up to five weeks' stock held in store. Improvements in inventory turnover during this period were relatively slight. The second stage, 'Depot Control', saw the establishment of retail RDCs in the early 1980s and the gradual transfer of stock and stock control from stores to the RDCs. Generally, orders were still taken on a weekly basis, but there were several deliveries made each week, and lead times were beginning to edge down. Stock levels were significantly reduced by this centralization process. The RDCs still operated on a put-away and let-down basis, with order pickers touring the picking face to assemble complete orders for branches on a pick-by-store basis. This period also saw the increasing introduction of computerized branch replenishment systems.

In the third stage, 'Head Office Control', the control of replenishment was transferred from the RDCs to retail head offices, with further increases in order review frequency and reductions in lead time. Stock in the system fell further, to between one and three weeks. A further innovation was the initial introduction of ordering based on data obtained from the checkout scanners. The new concept of composite, multi-temperature storage and distribution began to appear.

In the United Kingdom, retail grocers are already in the final stage, 'Just-In-Time', for perishable goods and are fast moving there for frozen and non-perishable packaged grocery products. Here, there can only be a final step change as RDC stock is reduced to the minimum to support pick-by-line cross-docking. The features of this phase are the extension of the composite networks supported by accurately-timed, daily deliveries on very short lead times.

In summary, the period of this overall evolution features a centralization of warehousing, inventories and inventory control, coupled with a trend towards advanced JIT replenishment methods, supported by massive retail investments in information technology support.

By transferring the four stages of development to the x-axis, a generalized picture of distribution evolution may be obtained (see Figure 6.5). The state of development of a market in general or an

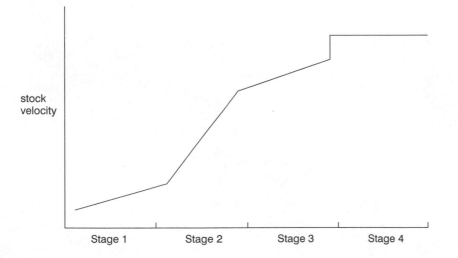

Figure 6.5 Distribution evolution

individual retailer in particular may be mapped on to this model by positioning them at the appropriate stage. However, fundamental to progress up this curve is the presence or absence of a number of the enabling technologies illustrated in Figure 6.6.

In order to move from Stage 1 to Stage 2 and operate via an RDC, it is necessary for the RDC to have some sort of warehouse management system. For the inventory to be controlled at the RDC, an RDC level stock control needs to be introduced. The central-iszation of the control of inventories at Head Office requires central visibility of RDC stocks and a process and system for managing them. To progress effectively to Stage 4, a retailer ideally needs the goods received to be bar-coded with the appropriate identifiers, as well as a computerized point-of-sale data capture system and computer-assisted store ordering processes. For the communications to work effectively, EDI links have to be established with suppliers. The significance of this simple model is that the enabling technologies up to the end of Stage 3 require only implementation by the retailer. There is no impact on the manufacturer. However, in order for a retailer to implement EDI and to scan bar-coded cases, his suppliers have to modify their own systems and processes to conform

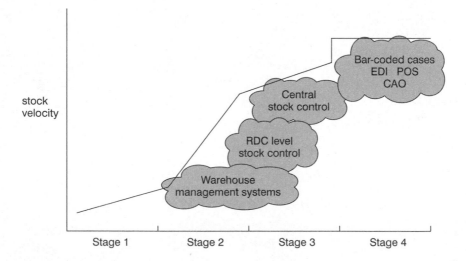

Figure 6.6 Prerequisite 'enabling' technologies

to these new requirements. This is a case of integration 'forced' on to a manufacturer as a requirement for doing business.

Another aspect of this evolution of replenishment processes is the concept of 'opportunity' technologies which can be introduced at various stages of the development curve. Figure 6.7 below illustrates this. Here it may be seen that Vendor Managed Inventory offers an opportunity for retailers still at Stage 2 in the evolution curve. Technologies such as cross-docking and automated goods-in vehicle scheduling at retail RDCs are increasingly propounded as methods of further driving down costs. However, each of these approaches demands a systems and business process change on the part of the other players in the supply chain. These will certainly generate one-off implementation costs and quite likely on-going operational cost increases for one partner which will not always outweigh the overall benefit, even though the initiator of the change may himself gain. These are further examples of integration as a means of gaining control or driving benefits for one party only.

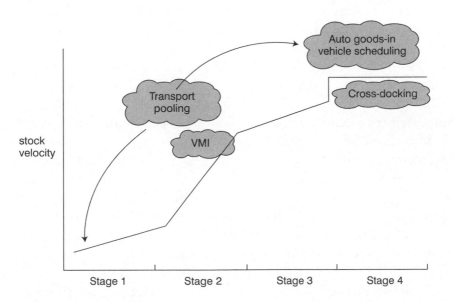

Figure 6.7 'Opportunity' technologies transport policy

EXAMPLE OF ACROSS-THE-CHAIN INTEGRATION

However, an example of an opportunity technology which can offer benefits across the whole of the evolution curve is transport pooling (see Figure 6.7), although this has to be based on cross-sectoral collaboration in which the day-to-day management is vested in disinterested third parties, rather than vested in any one supply chain partner. This is explored further below. Figures 6.8 to 6.13 illustrate the concept. In simple terms the supply chain is often viewed as a flow of information and goods between suppliers and retailers (Figure 6.8). In reality, there are many third parties involved in the chain, notably many separate transport and warehousing operators (Figure 6.9). On the basis that the use of opportunity technologies such as transport pooling derives greater benefit from a larger number of participants, then there are likely to be at least as many opportunities for consolidation *across* many supply chains as there are *along* single ones. Here, across the chain integration affords a genuine chance of optimization (Figure 6.10). However, complex communications and the absence of standards inhibit the achievement of synergy opportunities (Figure 6.11). For example, Figure 6.12 illustrates the communication flows that take place between the parties involved. In addition to the routine exchange of orders and invoice data between the supplier and customer head offices and, potentially, the exchange of warehouse stocks and issues data in a CRP relationship, there are many instructions issued between both the supplier and retailer and their logistics operators – transport movement instructions, warehouse order picking and assembly instructions, etc. Further, each haulier may have to make collection and delivery bookings at each warehouse. These instructions are not often issued in any sort of industry standard format, nor are they visible to other parties. The opportunity for improving synergy must stem from simplifying and standardizing these communications, using a third party added-value network service to act as a communications clearing house and a consolidation coordinator (Figure 6.13).

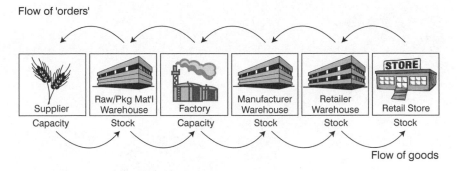

Figure 6.8 Supply chain characteristics

Figure 6.9 Networks of third parties

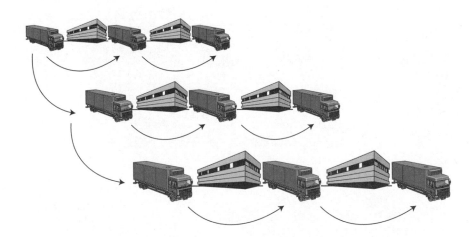

Figure 6.10 Consolidation opportunities along and across many supply chains

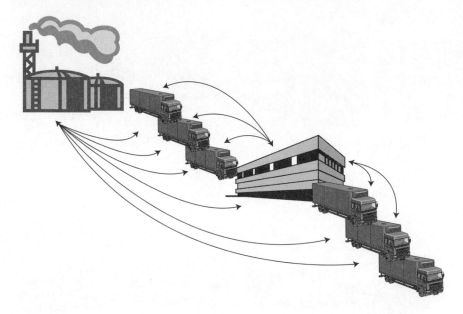

Figure 6.11 Complex communications via an added-value network service

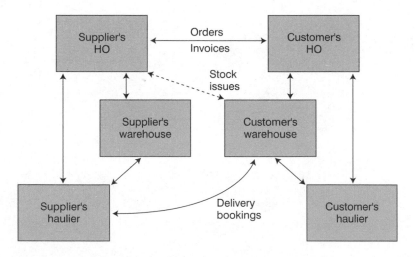

Figure 6.12 Replenishment interfaces

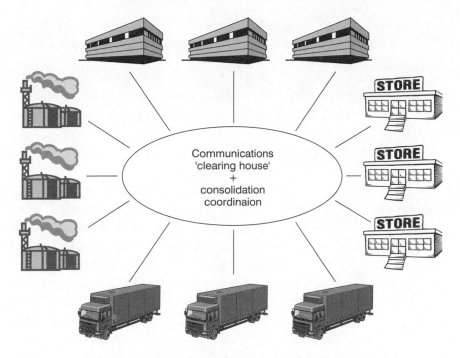

Figure 6.13 Simplified communications via an added-value network service.

Integration across the chain is thus about integrating replenishment processes with the other parties involved, such as transport and warehousing suppliers, and communicating with them via electronic means. This integration needs to address what processes should be included, what should be communicated, with whom, when, how and why, and how the activity should be organized to optimize its efficiency together with what new software and services will be needed to facilitate this way of working.

FACILITATING ACROSS-THE-CHAIN INTEGRATION

Current grocery industry logistics thinking across Europe is increasingly dominated by activity in ECR. Much of this is now retailer-led and, as is evident from the foregoing analysis, not always in the best interests of manufacturers. There are four principles which

133

should drive logistics development and ECR. These should aim to do the following:

1. To reduce total supply chain costs.
2. To enhance consumer value and community benefit.
3. To obtain an equitable division of any benefits resulting from change.
4. To maintain a fair balance of control in the supply chain.

The thesis explored above is that growing retailer power and significant retailing developments in internationalization, new store formats, own label, information technology and distribution are characterized by a trend towards not only centralization of control of their own supply chains by retailers but also attempts to acquire greater control over manufacturer supply logistics. Retailers are currently driving supply chain development towards their own goals and not always in the interests of the above principles. Their initiatives are sometimes detrimental to the interests of branded manufacturers (current 'best practice' ideas such as more frequent deliveries, cross-docking and pick by line are not necessarily in the best interests of the principles). There is a clear danger of transfer of control downstream and transfer of costs upstream. This situation may be redressed through promoting awareness of the real consequences and developing new initiatives rather than trying to redirect existing ones such as ECR. Hence there is a need to develop new initiatives in cost-effective distribution to the consumer. This can best be managed via a new collaborative approach. An outline of the objectives of collaboration and a method for establishing it is set out below.

A NEW COLLABORATIVE APPROACH

The broad principle here is that the greater the number of participants, the greater the synergy opportunities and the greater the chance of levering action within the logistics and network services provider community. By centralizing common activities and 'leapfrogging' the current thinking, this will also help to avoid the proliferation of multiple communication and operating standards which add costs. This is envisaged as operating within a free market environment in order to drive synergies and reduce redundancy, therefore leading to lower costs.

A collaborative approach between manufacturers, their suppliers and customers is envisaged, aimed at optimizing physical flows, executed via a community of service providers, working to common commercial principles. This could feature combined purchasing and operations in physical distribution and sharing of physical logistics resources. This would be supported by a common set of enabling systems and technologies, based upon common standards and a set of common cost measures. This will require an open, competitive market of a large number of service providers (logistics, finance, IT) covering all supply chain functions. (See Figures 6.14 and 6.15 below.)

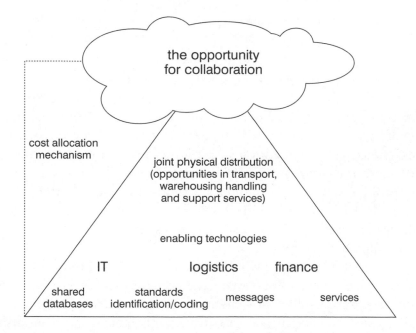

Figure 6.14 Opportunity for collaboration

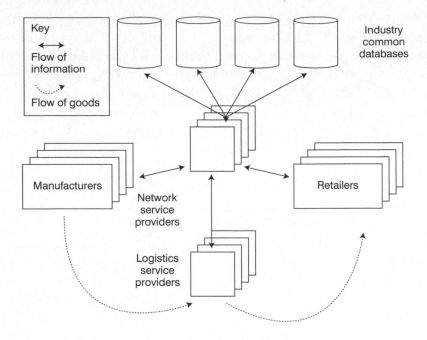

Figure 6.15 Open market solution

The approach to this collaboration is to establish a shared view on how best to achieve the principles above, to promote change to deliver the principles, to support only changes which support the principles and to resist changes which contravene them. The benefits of such collaboration would be that a free market approach fosters choice and competition and the common use of the service providers and common standards reduces redundancy and prevents the proliferation of multiple data formats. In addition, the opportunity for benefit grows with the number of participants and, overall, this is a better way to drive synergies and reduce supply chain costs equitably.

The service provider would manage the pooling of information and provide added value services, such as providing visibility and tracking of transport movements, optimizing transport circuits, managing the disposition of transport assets, consolidation activities, and returnables flows. In addition, central data base applications such as operational analyses and freight bill management could be offered.

PRINCIPLES FOR COLLABORATION

Members of such a working approach will need to obtain agreement on the vision, scope and objectives of collaboration, to develop common principles for commercial dealing and operations, and to build a shared terminology and working standards. They will need to be able to demonstrate consistency and sustainability of performance, transparency of information and mutual trust. Membership should be restricted to parties who have compatible physical characteristics in their supply chains (temperature, product compatibility – non-injurious characteristics such as odour taint). They must be prepared to pool information and be willing to change their current practices. They must be able to exchange data electronically and be prepared to commit both adequate business volumes to the joint enterprise and sufficient human resources to ensure successful participation.

OUTLINE METHOD FOR COLLABORATION

The methodology is based upon a matrix approach. This consists of first identifying focus areas for collaboration and then building a programme based on a number of process steps.

The focus areas are:

- commercial principles;
- network strategy;
- warehouse facilities;
- full vehicle trunking;
- store deliveries;
- IT support.

The process steps are:

- common mind-set;
- communications;
- development;
- planning;
- performance targets;
- performance evaluation;
- process effectiveness;
- continuous development.

Establishing a common mind-set is the process of understanding the mutual objectives of participating businesses. A communication channel and the processes for communication then need to be set up. The development stage is aimed at agreeing the programme of work within which mutual expectations and performance targets will be determined and the resources necessary for implementation and operation agreed. Operating performance needs to be reviewed frequently and appropriate adjustments made. The effectiveness of the process needs to be monitored regularly and a programme for continuous improvement run. The matrix may then be completed and a set of tasks confirmed for each cell (see Figure 6.16).

CONCLUSION

UK replenishment practice is in advance of much of the ECR theory and retailers are in the driving seat. Models of development trends may be built, on to which the position of suppliers and their customers may be mapped. The characteristic features of each stage

	Commercial Principles
Common mind-set	• Establish core principles for co-operation • Assess potential partners • Assess coherence of visions, style, approaches etc.

Figure 6.16 Template for collaboration

of each of these evolutionary models determine a number of prerequisite enabling technologies and consequential opportunity technologies. Such an approach can provide valuable insight into possible future retail developments. However, control of the supply chain has long been essential, for short shelf life and private label products. A source of retailers competitive advantage is the efficiency of 'their' supply chain across the total product range. Logistics efficiency via a single supply chain is therefore their main priority. Consumers judge retailer value (for stock-up shopping) across the total shopping basket but the presence of major brands is also a 'benchmark of value'. Thus multiple retailers will continue to press for control of the supply chain across their range, including packeted goods, and branded manufacturers must seek a mutually acceptable basis for supply chain development and operations with them in order to remain listed. Managing this together with handling the different supply chains of other trade channels to maximize availability efficiently is the key to growing consumer value.

Common terminology, measures and communication standards are fundamental to industry progress. Manufacturers must therefore focus on and clearly define the processes at the interfaces between their own and retailers' businesses. They must set up appropriate performance measures and build enabling systems to support the evolution of these interfaces. They must explore 'opportunity' technologies and their impacts and prerequisites and creatively re-engineer their use of assets and systems to lever the benefits of these opportunities. EDI should become a strategic thrust of doing business. This will require new EDI message exchanges and standards to be confirmed. Across the chain consolidation opportunities should be explored and wider support sought for such approaches.

There are a number of other implications for manufacturers: they must provide a variety of solutions for different channels and customers. They must have the skill, resources and information available to manage their category in-store, supported by activity-based costing to give internal (and possibly external) transparency to their cost structures. They need to be able to synchronize customer plans with their manufacturing and logistics capability. They must recognize the role of information and information technology in creating this new transparency and in enabling these new methods of working.

There needs to be a new integration of sales and market planning planning and logistics operations in which visible in-store activity planning can be linked to production scheduling and stock deployment. More responsive physical distribution networks need to be established which can accommodate lead-time compression with the appropriate capacity. Opportunities for resource sharing require the development of the necessary IT capability supported by EDI, traded unit and pallet bar-coding and conformity with standard industry data exchange formats. This should be underpinned by cost-related pricing based on activity-based costing. There needs to be clear communication of promotional activity, effective sales forecasting and clear, effective stock management policies supported by flexible manufacturing operations and advanced logistics capability, flexibility and efficiency.

Logistics service providers should be directly involved in the development of these opportunities. This will recognize the prevailing practice of using contract logistics and move the capability of the logistics industry forward by involving third party service companies in ECR initiatives to drive opportunities for synergy and consolidation. This will also increase the accessibility of efficient replenishment opportunities for smaller businesses. It will therefore require the development of standards in terminology, processes and messages between logistics service providers. A huge opportunity awaits the providers of value-added network service vendors in offering the communications infrastructure and management software to facilitate shared-resource operations.

In the United Kingdom the real future for the 'supply-side' component of ECR lies in rationalizing and revitalizing the approach to managing transport and consolidation on an industry basis. This will genuinely benefit all parties, including the consumer, but is dependent upon a radical rethink of the way the transport industry currently operates. Is the industry fit for the challenge?

7

THE EFFECTIVE IMPLEMENTATION OF CO-MANAGED INVENTORY (CMI)

Jane Winters

INTRODUCTION

Somerfield Stores had spent the last three or four years and millions of pounds investing in systems such as EPOS, depot and store replenishment systems and warehouse management systems, that would just allow them to catch up with their competition in the Grocery Retail sector. Having successfully implemented their supplier partnership programme with a number of major FMCG companies, which had resulted in supply chain benefits for both parties, Somerfield felt in a position to take the lead in some of the new inventory management techniques, rather than follow. Building upon the success of vendor management inventory (VMI) in the United States, Somerfield wanted to see whether VMI was a viable solution in the United Kingdom and quickly realized that the focus here would be more on co-operatively managing inventories by sharing data and information, rather than handing over total responsibility to the supplier.

Somerfield PLC sponsored the first significant multi-organizational trial of Co-Managed Inventory (CMI) in the United

Kingdom and possibly Europe. The trial was carried out from May 1995 to April 1996 with 12 leading suppliers of ambient, branded products, including several suppliers who compete in the same product category (see Table 7.1). Suppliers used a common CMI service solution (GE Information Services' POS*I) to forecast demand and replenish product into Somerfield's regional distribution centre (RDC) at Ross on Wye. Somerfield transmitted daily stock movement and stock on hand data to suppliers via standard EDI messaging in Edifact standard SLSRPT message (their first development of Edifact messaging). Somerfield also provided via e-mail links to the suppliers other *ad hoc* information such as promotional details including competitor promotional information and other market intelligence needed to create effective replenishment orders. Suppliers were then able to manage the forecasts which were NOT adjusted in any way by Somerfield.

Although POS*I is primarily a continuous replenishment system (CRP), three of the four main pillars of Efficient Consumer Response (ECR) were tested – Continuous Replenishment, Promotions Management and New Product Introduction. A key learning experience of the project was the recognition that these

Table 7.1 Supplier product profiles

Supplier	Product Categories	No of SKUs	% Promoted	Remarks
Bass	alcoholic drinks	25	28	
Britvic	soft drinks	20	10	excluding Robinsons
Cadbury	confectionery	77	30	highly seasonal
Chivers	preserves	25		price promotion only
Kelloggs	cereals	80	5–10	
Kraft	coffee and grocery	160	50	
Levers	laundry	77	15	
Lyons Tetley	tea	14	90	80s are 90% of volume
Nestle Rowntree	confectionery	80	15	excluding seasonal lines
Nestle Grocery	coffee and grocery	160	25–40	
Reckitts	household	80	10	
RHM	grocery	74	10	

techniques are interlinked, and that CRP alone is insufficient to achieve benefits from a VMI/CMI programme in the food grocery sector.

Somerfield set a service level performance target of 98.5 per cent, measured on case fill from Ross on Wye Regional Distribution Centre to store. Somerfield did not set any target inventory levels, but could measure the notional cost of excessive inventory. Focusing on depot to store service level rather than supplier to depot service level forced suppliers to be aware of the total supply chain and to think about consumer service rather than customer service. This was one of the several areas where the trial had started to prepare organizations to move towards the processes that will be required for the successful adoption of ECR in the future.

PHASES OF THE TRIAL

During May 1995 independent access to their individual environment on the CMI service was established for each supplier, and product data and demand history were loaded to create the initial forecasting models and product files. This allowed suppliers to familiarize themselves with the POS*I software and the processes required to run a CMI operation. All suppliers began a parallel run phase in July 1995. This phase was a formal evaluation of current real-world replenishment performance against the imaginary world performance of the CMI service. The objective of this phase was to allow the suppliers to build up sufficient confidence and skill in the processes and operation of a CMI service, and to demonstrate the potential stock management and service level benefits from the supplier operation and from the software, without the risk of live replenishment.

Performance of the suppliers using POS*I was measured against the real-world performance of Somerfield's inventory managers replenishing Ross on Wye RDC, using the depot to store service level and weeks stock cover as the measure. Regular review sessions were held during this phase, dependent upon the replenishment cycle (more frequent review for daily replenishment than for weekly replenishment). There was a major cultural and organizational benefit from working together, discussing results and issues, and agreeing solutions, as confidence grew and trust was built up in the potential of CMI.

From November 1995, suppliers began to cut over to a live replenishment operation, once they had satisfied Somerfield that the business and support processes were in place to allow the suppliers to manage the replenishment in Somerfield's Ross RDC (see Table 7.2). During this phase the performance in Ross on Wye RDC was measured against Somerfield's Bridgewater RDC which was similar in size and throughput to Ross, again using depot to store service level and weeks stock cover as the measure.

EXPERIENCES AND RESULTS OF LIVE RUNNING

Genuine hard and soft benefits were achieved during the trial, with a range of achievement across the product categories and suppliers (see Table 7.3). There is an indication that entry stock levels were between 10 and 30 per cent too high and the order pattern using CMI was able to drive down stock without compromising service levels. The factors affecting the degree of improvement were

Table 7.2 Duration of 'live' running operation

Supplier	Date of Live Running	No of Weeks Live
Bass	24/2/96	10
Britvic	13/4/96	3
Cadbury	13/1/96	15
Chivers	27/1/96	13
Kelloggs	25/11/95	23
Levers	24/2/96	10
Rowntree	10/2/96	12
Nestle Grocery	10/2/96	12
Reckitts	18/11/96	24
RHM	27/1/96	13

Note: Kraft Jacob Suchard and Lyons Tetley continued running in parallel mode throughout the trial, never achieving the live phase.

identified as frequency of replenishment and product profile. The majority of the suppliers were on a weekly replenishment cycle, which obviously limits the stock reduction potential. Total inventory (measured as number of weeks) tended to be driven up by promotional activity, push demand and stock allocation of promotional lines that creates some 'noise' in a pull demand oriented CRP system. No single supplier achieved spectacular gains in stock reduction or service level and we are convinced that this is because the major supply chain inefficiencies are not present in UK retail grocery that would allow the types of gains that were initially experienced with VMI programmes in the United States. Also the learning curve to achieve optimum performance by the suppliers ate away into a long period of the trial and suppliers did not start to see real improvements in performance until well into the trial period. Continued monitoring of the suppliers' performance after the trial end shows that greater benefits are now being achieved.

Several suppliers did experiment with different order patterns, replenishment frequencies and inventory planning parameters. Examples include:

- Raising target service level on 'A' class items from 98.5 per cent to 99.5 per cent.

Table 7.3 CMI trial performance statistics

Supplier	Wks Live	Avg Stock (Ross)	Avg S/L (Ross)	Avg Stock (B/W)	Avg S/L (B/W)	% Stock up (Down)	% S/L up (Down)
Bass	10	2.02	95.27	1.81	95.97	11.6	(0.70)
Cadbury	17	3.32	93.63	4.02	95.03	(17.4)	(1.40)
Chivers	14	2.13	99.01	2.04	96.53	4.4	2.48
Kellogg	23	1.78	98.67	2.00	99.07	(11.00)	(0.40)
Levers	10	1.96	93.88	3.27	92.43	(40.1)	1.45
Rowntree	12	2.66	94.66	3.25	92.26	(18.2)	2.20
Nestle	12	2.43	96.16	2.07	97.60	17.4	(1.44)
Reckitts	24	2.02	94.24	2.65	92.06	(23.8)	2.18
RHM	14	2.32	94.82	1.86	98.77	24.7	(3.95)

Note: Britvic also ran in live replenishment mode for three weeks, but this was insufficient data on which to establish an overall trend.

- Reviewing and amending replenishment multiples to align with rate of sale. Matching supply multiples to demand takes out demand peaks and lowers average inventory.
- Replenishment frequency – eg changing from weekly to twice weekly replenishment, but closely monitoring the additional supply chain costs at both Somerfield and the supplier, created by more frequent, smaller deliveries.
- Changing order pattern by consolidating their products from three groups to one group.

Major soft benefits were experienced by all of the trial suppliers as the following comments from one supplier acknowledge:

> As a model for Retailer/Supplier/Service Provider project, the trial has been outstanding. All parties have come together to work on a common problem and have produced the required results. There is now a first-class relationship between the retailer and the supplier and the shared data and extended view this gives of the supply chain mean a common understanding of the issues.

The key intangible benefits were universally seen as better communications and a greater understanding of the total supply chain. The trial also focused on the processes and procedures in promotions management and new product introduction. Both Somerfield and the suppliers have been able to improve their internal communications and understanding in this area to develop better processes. The trial also helped the participants to gain a better understanding of the organizational and cultural issues involved in implementing major business process changes. It has provided a framework which can be built upon to create subsequent ECR improvement programmes. It would now be seen as a big step backward to return to the old way of working where individual parts of the supply chain are owned and managed by individual companies and data and information are only used within those boundaries.

THE RESOURCE COSTS

The main element of operational costs for each supplier was manpower. The weekly load averaged out at four minutes per stock keeping unit (SKU) per week, in a range from 1.8 to 7.0. There was a rough inverse correlation between the time per SKU and relative supplier success. These resource requirements apply to one RDC, although it was projected that there would be economies of scale in managing all RDCs. Some of the manpower load was attributed to perceived lack of user friendliness of the POS*I application. Also some suppliers had no previous experience of creating replenishment so totally new skill sets had to be learnt and a long learning curve had to be overcome, whereas with other suppliers these skill sets were already in place either wholly or in part, giving less of a learning curve to go through.

Suppliers expressed concern about the future resource requirements, as the number of RDCs and retailers on CMI/ECR programmes increases. Suppliers indicated that it would be difficult to justify these additional resources unless the CMI financial benefits were shared and eventually a critical mass of customers on a CMI operation were achieved. It was also difficult to understand whether managing six depots would require six times the resource or whether this would be scaled down with each new depot.

OVERVIEW OF LESSONS LEARNT AND IMPLICATIONS

When CMI moves from a pilot phase into production, with replenishment to several RDCs or multiple retailers, then there are significant process changes. The project, which may have had a somewhat peripheral status within the supplier organization while it was a pilot, now needs to become more integrated with the standard supplier business processes and, ultimately, suppliers will seek to integrate CMI systems into upstream supply chain management systems.

Although some of the processes are different, we do not believe that CMI requires any major changes in the terms and conditions of doing business. Successful CMI programmes are built upon a basis of partnership, trust and timely and accurate information exchange, rather than on detailed legal contracts. There is an 'implied contract' with continuous replenishment programmes. Since the supplier is now responsible for the time-phased replenishment, suppliers MUST have the stock available and may have to prioritize stock for CMI customers. Retailers must allow suppliers to deliver in accordance with the CMI system replenishment schedule, so in principle CMI suppliers should be given priority in warehouse delivery slot bookings.

Where processes have changed (eg responsibility transferred from retailer to supplier), then both parties have to document how the new processes are expected to work, including a risk assessment and contingency plan for managing those risks. It is, however, also worth bearing in mind that where total supply chain costs have been reduced through these practices, negotiation will need to take place with the commercial areas of both businesses to agree how these savings should be shared.

In the trial, supplier companies organized their activities in a number of different ways. The most successful suppliers organized the CMI project as a logistics or supply chain development project and were able to set up a cross-functional team under a strong business project manager with dedicated resources throughout the trial period. The cross-functional teams typically had forecasting AND inventory management representation and expertise, and often the same people would be responsible for both functions. IS and sales/marketing input were represented in the successful teams, but did not play a dominant role.

The less successful organizations were those who were unable or unwilling to organize the project as a logistics or supply chain development project with a cross-functional team. Suppliers without a strong logistics supply chain structure tended to run the project from the trading/commercial function, and often had forecasting and inventory management resources split between separate departments. One supplier organized the project with the inventory and forecasting roles being operated not only from different functions within the business but also from different divisions of the business that were geographically 200 miles apart.

Suppliers who were unable to commit the appropriate resources to the project were less successful, and tended to get bogged down with systems issues rather than focusing on the operational processes. The most serious lack of resource was where suppliers lacked a strong hands-on project manager. Several supplier CMI projects were delayed by changing their teams midway through the pilot, with a consequent learning curve for the new team. However, this did have a positive effect ultimately, where the new teams were empowered and focused, and several suppliers made very quick progress once they had reorganized along cross-functional lines. One supplier, due to a major lack of resources throughout the pilot, forced the project back into the business as a day-to-day process, taking away the project focus and resulting in very poor performance.

The choice of a common system solution for all suppliers was only possible because it was a retailer-sponsored trial. This gave the opportunity for all suppliers to start the trial at the same time, without the need for expensive and time-consuming systems development. It was also used as an opportunity for GE Information Services to become part of the trial and use it as an opportunity to learn what the UK requirements would be for a CMI solution.

As our perception of CMI evolved towards an ECR-oriented view, it became clear that a CRP-type solution (whether service or in-house) was not sufficient. A very flexible system is needed which can handle both push and pull product demand, and which supports the most common ECR functions – in particular, strong promotions and event management, category management, and new product introductions. It is unlikely that this functionality will be found in a single application package. For some suppliers much of the systems benefit and value of a CMI operation may lie in receiving the daily stock movement information via standard EDI messaging and processing it using existing systems.

Organizations that succeed in ECR will do so because they are 'good' at supply chain management rather than technology. CMI and ECR projects have tremendous cross-functional business implications. The characteristics of a 'good' supplier CMI programme are as follows:

- Top management commitment, with a powerful business sponsor (possibly backed by an ECR steering committee or similar).
- Empowered cross-functional team culture with existing logistics or supply chain function.
- Strong hands-on project management, ideally reporting to a logistics development or logistics operation function (not led by IS or sales or marketing).
- Forecasting and inventory management seen as logistics or supply chain functions, with appropriate representatives as core members of the project team.
- IS and sales or marketing backing for the project (via steering committee) but CMI project manager obtains IS and sales or marketing input and resources as required during the trial.
- Pilot project run by core stable CMI team will use pilot phase to establish new internal and external business processes and support systems.
- Handover CMI operation in post-pilot phase to established operational functions within logistics/supply chain functions.

CRITICAL SUCCESS FACTORS AND RECOMMENDATIONS

From the learning experiences gained in the Somerfield pilot, we would summarize the characteristics of a successful VMI/CMI programme under the following headings:

- quality and depth of existing relationship;
- clear vision and objectives;
- organization and culture;
- choosing the right mix of products, CMI techniques and systems.

Quality and depth of existing relationship

It is obvious that suppliers and retailers must have a good existing relationship to undertake CMI successfully as there must be a high degree of trust. The relationship must be intelligent, mature and non-adversarial (even if this falls short of a formal partnership) and both parties must be willing to share both information and benefits.

Clear vision and objectives

As with any major change programmes, introducing CMI requires top management support and commitment on both sides. It is a business issue and certainly not a technology issue. An initial R&D or pilot phase is highly recommended, to lower the risk and to build up the necessary trust and confidence and to define the process and systems requirements. The service supplier may be able to provide a facilitative role, as GE did in the Somerfield trial. Pilots should be of limited length and be seen as phase 1 of a multiphase programme.

Improvement goals and measurements should be realistic and performance measurements should be made in a mutually agreed and understood way. Benchmarking current or historic supplier performance against the CMI measurement factors is essential for comparisons of CMI versus non-CMI performance.

Organization and culture

Prospective CMI/ECR participants should seek mature and stable partners who exhibit the following types of organization and culture:

- open and responsive;
- proactive, innovative and willing to make changes;
- willing to take risks;
- open to sharing information with partners and with competitors in a controlled way;
- business process perspective;
- empowered individuals;
- able to invest both money and resources in CMI programmes.

151

CMI pilot trials should start with a limited number of participants and products. It is important to choose the right partners and get the processes and issues sorted out before moving on to the majority.

For a retailer-sponsored hub, we would recommend that there should be no more than five suppliers in the pilot phase. There are significant diseconomies of scale above this number.

For the supplier, the number of products (SKUs) is a critical factor. Less than 50 SKUs is ideal, while 100 is manageable. Over 100 SKUs leads to a lack of clarity which clouds the real issues and makes these difficult to resolve.

Choosing the right mix of products, CMI techniques and systems

Some products are more suited to certain CMI techniques than others; therefore, if the objective is to trial CRP, then the product mix should be suitable for CRP; conversely, if the product mix is not entirely suitable, then other CMI techniques will be required, for example, a mix of solutions for push demand and pull demand models.

Exchanging accurate, complete and timely data is of critical importance to the success of a CMI programme. However, much of the data held by retailers on suppliers' products is incomplete or incorrectly coded. Front end data inspection for quality and source is a valuable activity and will save time in dealing with exceptions later. Constant dialogue between parties is also essential when product data changes occur to ensure that data integrity is maintained.

Entering into a CMI programme will shine a spotlight on all related supply chain systems and business processes and on the way that data and information are exchanged. This gives a great opportunity to both sides to tighten up the current processes and benefits not only the CMI operation but other areas of the businesses.

In terms of a distribution strategy, this should be DC and not store-based and ideally forecasting using consumer EPOS data. Both retailers and suppliers also need to have a reasonably mature electronic trading infrastructure in place to consider CMI.

NEXT STEPS

The pilot trial ended formally on 30 April 1996. It is the intention of Somerfield and the majority of suppliers to continue with the CMI-based operations. The natural evolution will be to build on the CMI pilot programme characteristics as follows:

- retailer-sponsored;
- community project;
- common service-based CRP-oriented solution;
- research and development focus;
- single RDC.

This should develop into a series of individual ECR improvement programmes with each supplier, tailored to meet the individual needs of that particular supply chain, with the following characteristics:

- joint agreement on improvement goals in the total Somerfield supply chain;
- supplier-selected, flexible systems solutions, with backward integration into suppliers' own business systems;
- probably different techniques and systems for management of pull demand vs. push demand;
- focus on wider ECR techniques, not just CRP;
- operational focus;
- multiple RDCs.

Some suppliers plan to position the Somerfield activities within a broader supplier-sponsored CMI programme, with proactive approaches to other retailers and wholesalers and upstream in the supply chain with their own suppliers. Somerfield will also look to start CMI with other suppliers using the selection criteria gained from the trial findings.

The CMI pilot has created an excellent framework for Somerfield and its suppliers to build on; it offers an opportunity to work together in joint management and optimization of the total supply chain and thereby achieve the goal of ECR: 'Working together to fulfil *consumer* wishes better, faster and at less cost'.

8

LOGISTICS IN TESCO: PAST, PRESENT AND FUTURE

David Smith

INTRODUCTION

Food retailing in the 1980s and 1990s has undergone a massive transformation. The most visible effects of this are the food superstores in the 1980s on which many food shopping trips are based and the return to a range of smaller formats in 1990s. The performance of the operations that underpin the retail outlets is vital. This chapter takes one such operation, the distribution process in one such company, Tesco plc, to illustrate how the retail 'revolution' has also been a distribution revolution.

BEHIND THE RETAIL REVOLUTION IS A DISTRIBUTION REVOLUTION

Retailing has been relatively neglected as a subject of academic study, despite its importance in the economy as a provider of both goods and jobs. It is apparent that components of the 'retail revolution' (Gardner and Sheppard, 1989) are worthy of detailed study, and one such component is physical distribution. While changes in retail location, outlet size, design and product range are obvious in a visual sense to consumers and academics alike, the development in distribution underpinning these retail changes is less apparent and less well understood.

This chapter aims to explain and account for the changes in physical distribution in food retailing. It develops earlier work both broadly (eg McKinnon, 1989; Fernie, 1990; Fernie, 1997) and specifically (eg Sparks, 1986) by examining general changes in distribution, before focusing in particular on how one company, Tesco plc, has transformed its distribution operations in order to satisfy modern consumer and retail demands. The chapter argues that change has, and will continue to have, an effect on corporate operations as well as on consumers and manufacturers. The Tesco plc Annual Report for 1991 states:

> *The transformation of Tesco from a price-driven retailer into an integrated group of the highest quality has been measured, discussed and commented on all along the way. We could probably say that there has never been a more public repositioning of a company's image than ours.*
>
> *(p 20)*

However, for many consumers, commentators and academics, the crucial distribution transformation that underpins change is unrecognized.

THE CHALLENGES FOR DISTRIBUTION

The retail responses (Dawson and Sparks, 1985) to the consumer and societal trends above require changes to the physical distribution strategy and operations of retailers. Table 8.1 links the earlier discussion of consumer effects of these responses. Each of these can be considered in turn.

The increase in store size that has occurred has seen the majority of food retailing concentrated on large superstores and

Table 8.1 Distribution effects of consumer, societal and retail change

Consumer, Societal Change	Retail Change	Distribution Effects
consumption	store size	vehicle scheduling and volumes
consumer behaviour	location	ease of distribution
shopping behaviour	own brands	control of distribution
individuals	product extension	distribution complexity, specialist handling
groups	finance	cost of distribution
society	service/value	need for consistent high-quality distribution
	technology	control by information

Source: Smith and Sparks, 1993

supermarkets. The increase in scale of units has brought increased vehicle requirements at such stores and the need to handle larger volumes of a wider range of products. As the stores increased in size, so the complexity of the back door increased and the potential for congestion and disturbance has been enhanced. The effect on distribution has been to force consideration of vehicle scheduling and how best to manage the large volumes needed by a modern superstore.

Concomitant with the rise of the unit size has been the movement of such stores to off-centre locations. The movement away from the high streets has improved the distribution position in many cases. The new stores are located in off-centre locations, generally with good road access. Their newness means that in many cases they have been built with modern distribution requirements in mind. This has eased the problems of distribution. However, the increase in unit sizes and ranges means that congestion and volume handling remain problems, even at off-centre sites. A modern food superstore in an off-centre location has a very different physical distribution requirement from the stores it replaces, even where the replaced store is a first or second generation superstore rather than a number of small stores.

The retailer development of own brands has clear distribution effects. Since own brands are within the control of retailers for longer than manufacturer brands, closer control can be exercised throughout the distribution channel. Food retailers have invested heavily in food technology and product development (Senker, 1989) and encouraged technological change in suppliers (eg Walsh, 1991). This is well demonstrated by the detailed involvement that Marks and Spencer and Tesco, for example, have with their suppliers and represents the movement from a physical distribution to a logistics orientation. Such involvement, particularly in own-brand development, provides distribution savings by better knowledge, information and co-ordination in the distribution channel. If a retailer has an own brand strategy, then manufacturer brands often have a greater battle to obtain shelf space. Individual manufacturers can gain by accurate adherence to delivery schedules and standards set by the retailers. Accurate and effective physical distribution thus becomes a competitive weapon for the manufacturers.

Own brands have been developed in existing and new product sectors. Product extension has been generated by consumer and technological changes. The development of frozen and chilled products exemplifies these interrelationships, as does the introduction of microwave cooked products. The development of new product types has increased the complexity of retail distribution. In many cases, the initial response was to allow specialist distribution companies to set up distribution channels for these products. More recently, however, there has been a re-integration of such channels with the core grocery products, although the need for specialist handling has increased rather than decreased. The food industry as a whole has been heavily involved in legislation such as the Food Hygiene Act and throughout the distribution channel there are requirements on product handling. This is most apparent where products require special temperature environments.

Finance is a key part of retailing and with stores becoming more and more expensive, attention has turned to the costs of distribution. This has taken a number of dimensions. The actual costs of the distribution activity have come under close scrutiny as their true nature is now being revealed by better accounting and finance information systems. At a simple level therefore distribution has to justify its expense. Obtaining the most effective system possible is a reasonable goal. However, distribution is also affected by the need to maximize selling space and avoid large distribution areas within stores. The stock therefore has to be held away from the retail location which places a premium on effective and consistent distribution. At the same time, stock holding can be expensive and wasteful and can hide proper consumer demand. The aim is to eliminate as much as is consistent with maintaining an appropriate service level. Purpose-built distribution centres themselves are expensive and retailers are concerned to make the best use of these costly facilities.

As has been indicated earlier, service and quality expectations held by the majority of consumers have increased. The need for distribution is therefore to perform the distribution activities at a 'consistently high quality level'. The move to centralize management and control is associated with the emergence of strategic planning and the adoption of a systems approach to retail operations, arising from these new management leading retailers. As these strategies imply a better focus on the consumer, so distribution operations and strategy underpinning the corporate strategies have had to change to reflect this focus. Distribution strategy has become an important element of corporate strategy (Walters, 1988; Gattorna and Walters, 1996; Christopher, 1997). Most strategies in food retailing focus on service and quality and thus the distribution quality must match the retail offering. The whole ethos of better service and customer care, however, means little if physical distribution is unable to get the foods to the shop in the right conditions, sizes etc, and at the right time. Managing the retail environment and pleasing the consumer also implies better management of the distribution process and channels.

Finally, retailers have introduced a substantial amount of technology into their operations at both store and head office levels and this has had major implication for distribution. Technology is enabling management control to remain effective in large stores and in chains of small stores. Laser scanning and computer control centres are becoming standard in warehouses and distribution centres with replenishment orders from stores transmitted electronically.

Communications and payment between retailers and suppliers are increasingly via electronic-data interchange such as Tradanet (eg McKinnon, 1990; Hendry, 1995). The important point to note is the increase in control of all aspects of operation that is offered by technological data collection, transmission and interpretation. Technology is being applied throughout the distribution channel to facilitate rapid and accurate information flows and thus timely and appropriate product distribution. As illustrations, Walter (1988) and Belussi (1987) provide detail on the importance of technology for Benetton in linking retail sales, distribution and production. Distribution is now a part of retailing that is controlled by information rather than by just doing.

Following on from technology introduction at the point of sale is the better matching of products and product availability to consumer desires and needs. Examples abound, particularly but not solely in the fashion trade, of how technology is being used to ensure that the retailer is stocking in the store what is selling rather than what the retailer hopes will sell. Retail buying and merchandising retain elements of retail knowledge and risk taking but increasingly consumer behaviour patterns are used to channel the knowledge and help decision-making. Merchandising and buying are becoming increasingly dependent on information technology assistance and this also then impacts on distribution practices, taking account of local variations.

The discussion above has demonstrated the range of effects and pressures that have faced retail distribution due to the changes in consumers, society in general and retailing. In addition to the effects noted above, it is also apparent that, as companies have grown bigger and become more successful, so the requirements of the distribution function have increased and the pressures, in terms of consistency and quality of performance, on running a multi-locational system have expanded. Stock has to be controlled not only in a horizontal dimension but also in a vertical dimension within the distribution channel. The managerial task in achieving this has become harder and more complicated as a result of the changes discussed above.

The main distribution responses to the managerial complexities have involved centralization and sub-contracting. Centralization has involved the replacement of multiple stock-holding points by one larger stock-holding point. For example, the back-rooms of many retail outlets can be replaced by a centralized distribution centre. This centralization saves valuable retail land from being used as storage facilities but also allows the flow of products to be regulated to the stores. There are thus operational and control reasons why centralization has been an attractive option. At the same time this move to centralize facilities has allowed the subcontracting of distribution to be contemplated. Distribution specialists often merchandise for food retailers but they have now taken over many core operations. There are arguments for and against contract distribution, but it has allowed food retailers to avoid human resource problems, finance issues and offer specialist major expansion of the role of distribution contractors in food retailing's centralized distribution.

In the same way as retailing has become more centralized, so too has the distribution specialist market. The effect has been to have a great deal of distribution activity organized among a handful of large companies at the various stages of the distribution channel. This exchange among large companies has increasingly become computerized and electronic in nature. Electronic links promote closeness in the distribution channel and yet flexibility and shared forward planning can become more common. In this way the service and cost trade-offs can be better organized and a more effective and efficient distribution system is developed. The changes in distribution operations as a consequence of the changes outlined above can be illustrated through the extended discussion of physical distribution in Tesco.

PAST: DOWNSTREAM DISTRIBUTION

The development of Tesco is well documented through journalistic accounts of the company's history (Corina, 1971; Powell, 1991). Tesco is Britain's number one food retailer and Europe's number one with annual sales of over £14bn in 1997–98 from over 10 million sq ft of sales area. Most of this sales area is in the form of 'conforming' superstores ie off-centre, large, single-storey buildings with associated free ground-level car parking. Over 75 per cent of profits come from such stores. A conforming store stocks more than 16 000 products across all major product groups in food and grocery. While mostly self-service, counter service is provided for departments such as delicatessen and fresh fish and other in-store departments eg Bakery. Over 50 per cent of products are own brand with a particular own-brand emphasis in fresh food.

This view of Tesco is, however, far removed from the origins of the company. Tesco made its name by the operation of a 'pile it high, sell it cheap' approach to food retailing. Price competitiveness was critical to this and fitted well with the consumer requirements of the time. The growth of the company saw expansion throughout the post-war period until the early 1970s. The approach to retailing epitomized by Sir Jack Cohen was put under pressure at this time as competition and consumer values altered.

1970S: OPERATION CHECKOUT AND AMBIENT CENTRALIZATION

Since the heyday of the era of 'pile it high, sell it cheap' the number of stores has decreased, while the average size of store has risen. This has involved a transformation of the store portfolio into several formats: superstore, market town, metro and express. Tesco emphasizes high quality, freshness and responsiveness to the customer. By keeping in close touch with its consumers, Tesco argue that they can provide better for their changing needs and wants. Their strategy has been to invest in about 20 major new stores each year. There has been enormous increase in the scale of the business between the 1960s and the late 1990s. The boost to turnover began in 1977 when the company, through Operation Checkout (Akehurst, 1984), stopped giving trading stamps, cut prices by 4 per cent but also started to move up-market. From 1985 onwards the net margin and thus profitability have been driven higher as the new Tesco took over and business efficiency gains have occurred.

The changes the customer sees are obviously focused at the store, but behind the store revolution and the changing store portfolio (location, scale, type, age) lies a distribution transformation without which the success of the 1980s and 1990s could not have been achieved and the base for the next millennium would be insufficient.

The distribution policies and strategies of Tesco have been the subject of previous study. This chapter extends this earlier work (Sparks, 1986, 1988; Smith and Sparks, 1993). There have been five main phases in distribution strategy and operation. First, there was a period primarily of direct delivery by the supplier to the retail store. Second, there was the move, starting in the 1970s, to centralized regional distribution centres for ambient goods and the refinement of that process of centralized distribution; it is this phase that has received most attention. Third, there has been the development of composite distribution starting in 1989. Fourth, the advent of retail vertical control up the distribution chain into primary distribution in the 1990s. Fifth, the application of retail horizontal collaboration with other companies to achieve better operating efficiency.

The Tesco distribution system in the 1970s in the wake of Operation Checkout (Akehurst, 1984) almost came to a halt. The volume of goods being moved by Tesco proved too large to handle in the timescales required. As Powell comments, quoting Sir Ian MacLaurin:

> *Ultimately our business is about getting our goods to our stores in sufficient quantities to meet our customers' demands. Without being able to do that efficiently, we aren't in business, and Checkout stretched our resources to the limit. Eighty per cent of all our supplies were coming direct from manufacturers, and unless we'd sorted out our distribution problems there was a very real danger that we would have become a laughing stock for promoting cuts on lines that we couldn't even deliver. It was a close-run thing.*
> *(Powell, 1991:184)*

Powell continues:

> *How close is now a matter of legend: outside suppliers having to wait for up to twenty-four hours to deliver at Tesco's centres; of stock checks being conducted in the open air; of Tesco's four obsolescent warehouses, and the company's transport fleet working to around-the-clock, seven-day schedule. And as the problems lived off one another, and as customers waited for the emptied shelves to be refilled, so the tailback lengthened around the stores, delays of five to six hours becoming commonplace.* Possibly for the first time in its history, the company recognised that it was as much in the business of distribution as of retailing.
>
> *(1991: 184, emphasis added)*

Operation Checkout provided a short-term shock to the distribution system. There were major problems in handling the peak weeks and the increased volumes, but generally the company coped, albeit through running multi-shifts in the distribution centres. Having weathered the distribution effects of Operation Checkout, it became clear that other changes to distribution would be needed as the new business strategy took hold. In effect, by Operation Checkout and the move up-market that followed, Tesco were changing the mission, vision, strategy and culture of the company. This included distribution operations.

The decision was taken to move away from direct delivery to stores to centralization. The basis of this decision (in 1980) was the realization of the critical nature of range control on the operations. Tesco always had delivered some products centrally but the majority had come direct from manufacturers to stores. At its peak this reached a direct to store:warehouse ratio of 83:17. In addition to being inefficient for the store operations and being unable to cope flexibly with increased volumes and quality, the system allowed almost no control or standardization of the retail outlets and of store managers. Powell uses the euphemism of 'private enterprise' (1991:185) to describe the pricing and stocking behaviour of individual store managers. With direct to store delivery, managers were 'encouraged' to 'buy-in' extra products on secondary lines to cover stock losses. The realization of the effects this was having on the business forced the decision to end buying in and managers' deal books and allowed the introduction of true stock results and range control. Centralization of control was established for the modern business. Tesco head office had to have this control if the company was to be transformed: centralized distribution was one plank in the control strategy.

Tesco adopted a centrally controlled distribution service (Kirkwood, 1984a, 1984b) delivering the vast majority of stores' needs, utilizing common handling systems, with deliveries within a lead time of a maximum of 48 hours (Sparks, 1986). Six key areas of this strategy can be identified. First, there was an extension and change to the existing fixed distribution facilities, including the building of new distribution centres. The location of these facilities was aimed at more closely matching distribution needs to the store location profile and to changes in this profile. Second, lead times improved. Improvements in technology allowed faster stock turn, allied to which was the scheduling of vehicles at all points in the channel. Third, common handling systems were used at the distribution centres and stores to handle stock replenishment more easily. Fourth, the demands of modern retailing required multi-shift working. Fifth, computer software modelled company decisions, allowing the best use of all facilities. Sixth, dedicated ie contract distribution was used to meet high levels of performance. The standards are set by Tesco and monitored by them. The contractors have to meet these specifications.

The effect of this strategy for Tesco has been to produce a more rationalized network of distribution centres, which are linked by computer to stores via head office. The proliferation of back-up stock-holding points has been reduced. These centres were the hubs of the network, being larger, handling more stock, more vehicles and requiring more efficient organization. Control of the system ensures the stores obtain the goods they require. The technology enabled this control, which in turn shaped the business strategy. The implications of these changes were to alter the spatial locations of the physical distribution structure and alter the transport patterns.

Tesco have handled dry grocery and non-food products via centralized distribution for a number of years. Many developments were made during the 1980s. For example, in 1983–84 Tesco moved from wooden pallets to roll cages and from a basic to a modern computer warehouse system (Dallas) which provides computer-controlled allocation of warehouse space and computer-calculated real-time bonus for productivity. Since 1984 the percentage of sales via central warehouses has increased from under 30 per cent to over 93 per cent.

ELECTRONIC DATA INTERCHANGE (EDI) AND COMPUTER DATA FLOWS AND DEVELOPMENTS

The composite centres are linked by computer to head office to pass product demand and the data to monitor and control the operation. For all products handled by the composite centres, forecasts of demand are produced and transmitted to suppliers. Composite distribution operates with no stockholding of the fresh products. The aim of the system is to allow suppliers to have a basis for preparing products. This is particularly important for short-life products where the aim is to operate a demand pull, just-in-time system from factory through the composite centre to the store. To meet such targets on delivery, each supplier needs information on predicted replenishment schedules.

This sharing of information is part of a wider introduction of electronic trading to Tesco. In particular, Tesco built a Tradanet community with suppliers (Edwards and Gray, 1990; INS, 1991) for both direct to store and distribution centre deliveries. This provided a number of benefits. Improvements to scanning in stores and the introduction of sales-based ordering have enabled Tesco better to understand and manage ordering and replenishment. Sales-based ordering automatically calculates store replenishment requirements based on item sales and generates orders for delivery to stores within 24 to 48 hours. This information is used via Tradanet to help suppliers plan ahead both in product and distribution. Delivery notes, invoices and other documentation including e-mail can also be sent by Tradanet. An INS report, quoting Tesco, states:

> *This represents a further reduction in stockholding without any drop in service levels. Indeed the service often improves because suppliers are no longer dependent purely on their own forecasting – there are fewer surprises and we are developing a better understanding of each other's business.*
>
> *(INS, 1991:4)*

1980s: COMPOSITE AND CONTRACT DISTRIBUTION

In 1989 Tesco had 42 depots in total, of which 26 were temperature-controlled. That in itself was a massive reduction from the plethora of small locations (including back-ups) found in the 1960s and 1970s, but was still capable of improvement. Fresh foods were basically handled through single temperature, single-product depots. These were small, inefficient and only used for part of the day. Tesco had reviewed the service the network gave the stores and implemented improvements in all product areas in 1986 and 1987. This meant, for example, in the short-life provisions network, that the stores received more frequent deliveries from a rationalized number of depots (from eleven to six). Investment was made in the Dallas computer system in the frozen depots and accounting and budget changes allowed a more accurate idea of the cost of distribution.

The tactics in the late 1980s were to make as many improvements as possible in order to give the stores a better service. But, there were still some disadvantages of the network. First, each product group had different ordering systems. Some were designed by the distribution contractor for their general use and not sympathetic to Tesco needs. This complicated distribution. Second, with so many sites it was prohibitively expensive to have on-site Tesco quality control inspection at each location. This meant that the standards of quality desired could not be rigorously controlled at the point of distribution. Third, because only single-product groups were handled, each store's delivery volume was low. Hence, it was not economic to deliver some products to all stores to maintain the best quality, as some goods require a temperature-controlled environment during delivery. As single products in warehouses they had to be carried on separate vehicles, which meant that five vehicles were needed to deliver the full range of products to each Tesco store. This added complication and congestion, and was costly. Fifth, it was realized that the network would neither cope with the growth Tesco forecast in the 1990s nor, as importantly, would it be ready to meet expected high legal standards on temperature control in the chill chain. These factors combined to revise the changes necessary to meet emerging operational requirements

The produce depot at Aztec West in Bristol was opened in 1986 and represented the best of the old network. Tesco could have made further investment in the traditional single-product distribution systems, upgraded the depot and transport temperature control and put in new computer systems, but would still have achieved overall a poor use of resources and therefore less than optimal cost efficiency. Tesco decided that they needed a new dimension in their distribution strategy to provide an upgraded service to stores for all their temperature-controlled products. The business strategy had moved on from the watershed of Operation Checkout to take advantage of the new quality-driven demands. The strategy of composite distribution was planned in the 1980s to take effect in the 1990s. A subsidiary requirement of this development was the importance of continuity of service during the changeover period from old to new so that the transition was seamless.

The major change to the centralization strategy as presented above was that the company now concentrated its distribution further by focusing on the development of the composite distribution network. Table 8.2 identifies the position before and after the introduction of the composite system.

Table 8.2 suggests that there is a more effective and transparent

Table 8.2 Impacts of composite distribution

Distribution Trends	Pre-composite	Post-composite
regional depots	single temperature and small in size	large and complex
centralization	about 70 per cent	increased to 85 per cent
stock holding	high in store	low in store and depot
delivery frequency	less than daily	daily
identify costs	some case rate	all costs known
chill chain control	single temperature	rigorous control for freshness
computerization	half telesales	total integration

Source: Smith and Sparks, 1993

system of distribution in place and that the total efficiency of the chain has improved. Composite distribution enables temperature-controlled products, chilled, fresh and frozen to be distributed through one system of multi-temperature warehouses and vehicles. Composite distribution used specially designed vehicles with temperature-controlled compartments to deliver any combination of these products. It provides daily deliveries of these products at the appropriate temperature so that the products reach the customers at the stores in the peak of freshness. The insulated composite trailer can be sectioned into one, two or three chambers by means of movable bulkheads. There is independent control for up to three temperature regimes. For example, frozen products at -20 degrees Celsius can be carried with fresh meat at +1 degree and bread and bananas at +12 degrees without affecting product quality. The size of each chamber can be varied to match the volume to be transported at each temperature. The composite distribution network now has nine centres, one of which, Southampton, has a sorting system. Centralizing distribution of these products in this way has reduced costs and improved sales and productivity through improved quality of product and service. These nine centres have replaced the 26 single temperature centres in the previous network.

Each of the nine distribution centres services a region of the country and approximately 60 stores. The sites are all close to key motorway intersections or junctions which allow rapid access. Of the nine composite centres, four are run by Tesco. The remainder are operated by specialist distribution companies, two by Wincanton, two by Exel Logistics and one by Hays. This mix enabled a comparison of performance of the Tesco centres and the subcontractors as a league table of performance.

Composite distribution provides a number of benefits. Some derive from the process of centralization of which composite distribution is an extension. Others are more directly attributable to the nature of composites. First, the move to daily deliveries of composite product groups to all stores in waves provides an opportunity to reduce the levels of stock held at the stores and indeed to reduce or obviate the need for storage facilities at store level. All short-life products are received by each composite distribution centre during the afternoon and evening and delivered to the stores before trading commences the next day. Tesco call this the first wave. Longer-life and ambient products which are stocked lines are delivered to stores on the second wave, which is between 8am and 10pm. All deliveries are made at prearranged times. Tesco composite distribution centres have achieved on-time delivery in excess of 95 per cent of occasions. They have done this despite adverse weather and traffic conditions. Given this operating procedure and performance level, the potential for stock reduction is clear. In aggregate terms, the changes in distribution stock position in the company have improved continuously. Over the 1980s, the changes have succeeded in halving the stock days in the system.

The second benefit of composites is improvement to quality with a consequent reduction in wastage. Products reach the store in a more desirable condition. Better forecasting systems minimize lost sales due to out-of-stocks. The introduction of sales-based ordering produces more accurate store orders and more rigorous application of code control results in longer shelf life on delivery, which in turn enables a reduction in wastage. This is of crucial importance to shoppers who demand better quality and fresher products. In addition, however, the tight control over the chain enables Tesco to satisfy and exceed the new legislation requirements on food safety.

Third, the introduction of composites provided an added

benefit in productivity terms. The economies of scale and enhanced use of equipment provide greater efficiency and an improved distribution service. Composite distribution means that one vehicle can be used instead of the five needed in the old network. The result is reduced capital costs and less congestion at the store. Within composites, changes such as inbound scanning and radio-linked computers on fork-lift trucks have further enhanced productivity. In essence, throughout the system there is an emphasis on maximizing productivity and efficiency of the operations.

The introduction of composites is not a simple procedure. Considerable problems were encountered and solved. This has involved close examination of costs which has enhanced the need to work closely with suppliers and distribution specialists. There are detailed performance measures which focus on the improvement of service and cost against which specialists are measured. Fundamentally, the move to composites has led to the centralization of more product groups, the reduction of stock holding and its faster movement up the channel, information sharing via Tradanet, the reduction of order lead times and better code control for critical products.

There are certain issues that exist even post-composite. First, the development of computerized systems takes a long time and is costly. Second, there is a need to maintain the continuity of service to retail which means that the implementation of improvements must be invisible to distribution's customer, the retail stores. Third, the cost of primary distribution remains within the buyer's gross margin and is not identified clearly and separately. This cost has had to be substantiated indirectly by talking to suppliers and hauliers. Finally and most importantly, certain sectors of the supplier base are fragmented and not fully organized to the needs of retail distribution. It is their fragmentation which makes the task of securing further permanent improvements difficult.

The most significant operational issue concerning suppliers centres on the gap between the ideal and the actual supplier delivery profiles during the day and the impact this was having on the punctuality of first-wave deliveries to the stores. The operators had to forecast the hourly patterns of their staff in order to organize them into correct shift patterns throughout the day. Other important but related issues were the motivation of the work-force during these changes, accurate planning for the peak week demand by hour through the busiest days and maximizing the use of capital investment in the warehouse and transport.

To address the problem of better scheduling deliveries to depots from suppliers, particularly fresh foods, detailed rotas were established to ensure that the composite centres did not receive all their products in a short time window at the end of the day. Close liaison and new methods of ranking products helped to overcome the problems of delivery compression. Thus, the productivity of the composites and the effective capacity of composite depots have increased.

PRESENT: UPSTREAM DISTRIBUTION

1990s: primary distribution: origins, opportunities and consolidation

Suppliers and manufacturers, logistics service providers and retailers work together in the supply chain and focus on the needs of the customer who purchases the product. In secondary distribution the industry had been successful with its focus on specific objectives.

By applying established skills, the operators handle higher volume throughput and achieved improved unit cost of moving goods to retail stores (see Figure 8.1). The trend is particularly significant because as well as absorbing inflation Tesco have made improvements in the service to retail. The business has shorter lead times, with more frequent and more punctual deliveries with orders transmitted by Electronic Data Interchange (EDI). This is the heritage and background to primary distribution which can be defined as: the physical movement of the goods from the despatch bay of the factory to goods in at the depot. It is the transport and any associated consolidation of goods from groups of suppliers.

The initial idea started in 1990. The purpose was to identify and

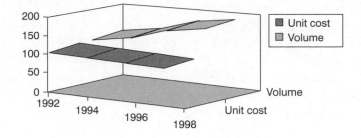

Figure 8.1 An Index of Volume and Unit Cost: 1992 base year

implement changes that were profitable to the whole supply chain, supplier, logistic service provider and retailer; to identify solutions in partnership with logistic service providers and suppliers that offered lowest cost for the supply chain as a whole and not just for one section at the expense of the others. Frequently this was a shared user solution, which is different from the dedicated solution found in secondary distribution where there is total visibility of costs. Primary distribution required a change in approach and style; Tesco had to let go of that direct control and allow the appointed hauliers and consolidators greater freedom with more empowerment over the shape of the solutions.

Traditionally Tesco have bought goods from suppliers at a delivered price. There was no visibility of the distribution element of the total cost of the product. Once the scale of the cost of primary distribution had been calculated, then there was a business motivation to apply logistics resources to identify opportunities to make improvements in the organization and structure of the inbound flow of goods. The purpose was to organize domestic UK, European and world-wide distribution networks based on analysis of those regions from which there was a high level of purchasing and the best centres of distribution excellence in those regions. Once this analysis was complete, it was then possible to appoint and set up primary networks in the United Kingdom, Europe and around the world. This was a second revolution in retail distribution but one that does not require much capital outlay; capital that was better directed to retail store development. Tesco were then able to be proactive in negotiating more competitive distribution rates as a result of the negotiation scale, the command of the sourcing of products and their expertise in distribution operations. These factors all contributed to enhanced operational efficiency and supply-chain profitability. There was a valuable cost contribution that could be made by involving the operators in identifying more efficient ways of organizing primary distribution and then helping bring those insights to the surface and create solutions that worked for all the segments of the supply chain. It was important to work in a cross-functional style within the different functions of Tesco: the buyers, supply chain, and distribution. The primary distribution managers sat in the commercial areas with which they were working, for example, the primary manager for produce sat among the produce buyers. This created a united focus on achieving good results for the business.

Total supply chain, pipeline distribution, 3D logistics, partnership and change of style

The relationship between the supplier, logistic service provider and retailer was focused to achieve a total supply-chain perspective from the supplier through to the consumer. This was called 3D logistics. Tesco appointed a Supply Chain Development Director with the broad objective of looking ahead three to five years and reporting to the Chief Executive. One of the objectives was to structure the hourly flow of goods both into and out of the distribution centres to create as big a capacity as possible without building more depots and balancing the capacity of primary and secondary distribution. This was called pipeline distribution.

An important part of this retailer and supplier relationship is the supplier collection programme within a depot's geographical delivery area. A supplier collection is where a Tesco vehicle collects product from a supplier on its way back to the depot following a store delivery. In the full 1996–97 year this saved 3 million miles of empty running which saved 4 600 tonnes of carbon dioxide

emission. In addition, there was the supplier onward delivery programme to the retail stores. This involved suppliers' vehicles which
had delivered to depots or were conveniently in the area taking
goods to Tesco retail stores on their way back to their base. In 1997
Tesco initiated the programme with a three-year target of achieving
the same level of benefit as supplier collection.

The drive towards partnership has required a change in skills.
One aspect that required some review covered decisions about
when to co-operate. There are three levels of collaboration that are
possible between companies: operational, middle management and
strategic. The most powerful is the strategic, where there is joint
agreement on areas of mutual importance. Within Tesco, the
Supply-Chain Development Director was involved with major suppliers about the future shape of the supply chain together with the
Commercial Directors who were increasingly focused on the importance of the long-term partnership with major suppliers for product
development and the scale of sourcing to support the growth of the
business. This created a new framework for the strategic discussions
with the logistic service providers.

This was new because traditionally the focus had been on the
two-way relationship: either the retailer with the supplier; or the
supplier with the logistic service provider. Tesco as a retailer viewed
the hauliers as the total responsibility of their suppliers. If there was
a problem with the delivery being short or late, then the retailer
would phone the supplier and expect them to address the remedy
with the haulier, rather than get involved in the details of the issue
that was their problem. The change was influenced by the realization that without the involvement of the retailer, many of the solutions could not be put in place; it required three-way collaboration.
Adopting such a partnership style with suppliers and the distribution industry became a conviction that is held deeply by the primary
distribution team in Tesco.

Once the principles of the strategic business relationship have
been agreed, then middle management can collaborate within specific functions. The most valuable were promotion planning, new
product development, forecasting peak trading volumes, electronic

data interchange, inventory management and exchanging informa-tion on the unit cost of distribution. The third level of collaboration is the operational focus on the efficiency of the day-to-day opera-tion and listening to the issues raised by the operators. For example, one of the biggest opportunities that can be unlocked is by exchang-ing information on the peak and slack periods of vehicle use. Businesses are interested in improving their return on the capital invested and in having the smallest size of core fleet to meet their needs. There are peaks and troughs in the volume of demand, with the result that there are periods in the week and even in the day or night when vehicles stand idle. Each company can only go so far in terms of its own efficiency. The next step change was by mutual col-laboration because by working together there was more that com-panies can achieve. Anything that helped to identify opportunities to take cost out of the primary distribution segment of the supply chain was a topic for the sharing of information and objectives.

The joint objective for the industry was to create the conditions in which the unit cost of primary distribution reduced year on year and, at the same time, the return on the capital invested in vehicles increased by better co-ordination and stronger confidence in the plan-ning information. The purpose was to identify and implement prof-itable change: profitable to the whole supply chain – supplier, distribution operator and Tesco. The result was an important strate-gic alliance between primary and secondary distribution that exam-ined the peaks and troughs in vehicle utilization to find where they were complementary. By using the advantage of the right sort of information, companies could act to their mutual benefit. One way of creating an opportunity was to examine the movement of equipment such as cages and trays which could release these other opportunities.

There was one particular aspect of this collaboration which had great potential. It was the onward delivery of assembled orders from the RDCs to the retail stores. It required some changes in trailer design. The dry freight trailer delivered goods on wooden pallets into the depots. If the distribution operator retro-fitted strapping equipment in the trailer to secure the cages of assembled stock, then it created the possibility of delivering to retail stores at peak times. This was not a new concept but it was proving to be one that was difficult to get the industry to implement. The industry needed to generate a critical mass of 1 500 such trailers. The application in the temperature-controlled environment required a bulk-head and a second evaporator. A critical mass of 500 was needed to generate confidence among the transport operators that the right equipment was available when it is needed. They had to depend on this in their transport operations.

FUTURE ISSUES

There are several trends which will be important drivers of change at the start of the next millennium such as the impact of home shopping; the use of rail for continental sourcing; full data links with suppliers; 'green' distribution to meet environmental concerns and the whole arena of horizontal integration. These are already visible in the late 1990s and indicate the kinds of issues that companies will include as part of their logistics strategy.

Horizontal integration

Already valuable improvements had been achieved through a strategic alliance between operators in primary and secondary distribution. This was also visible in shared use of warehouse and transport resources in primary distribution. There was a benefit to the supplier who, if desired, could still deal with one logistic service provider for all his retail customers. This went further with companies collaborating and exchanging routes where there were complementary loads and capacity. This all demonstrates that the supply chain can provide opportunities to reduce costs for all segments without a company losing competitive advantage. That competition takes place on the retail shelves. Consistent feedback from suppliers points to benefits for all by removing the complexity. As a result, there is collaboration through the industry association, the Institute of Grocery Distribution (IGD), so that major retailers can work together on an industry standard. One good example of this is the design of the returnable plastic tray. Another example is the open top cardboard box for fruit and vegetables. Although pallets of a single product interstack safely at the suppliers, when these different products from different suppliers and from different companies from different countries arrive at composites they do not interstack with each other when the store order is assembled. The industry is working through this to agree an industry standard for the essential features that will enable these different boxes to interstack. This links with the ECR Europe Efficient Unit Loads (EUL) project which identified over a thousand variants of cardboard box and made recommendations about modular sizes that fit both the euro-pallet and the 1000 x 1200 mm pallet used in Britain.

Environment

The environment is a topic which has increased in importance in the 1990s. There are two aspects to this topic: air quality and global warming. The first concerns the impact on air quality and health from vehicle emissions. For freight which uses diesel it is about using a low sulphur fuel with a tray to catch the particulates. The measurements are taken at a series of kerbside locations and it will be high priority to achieve the agreed targets. The second has its origins in the Rio summit when governments agreed to take action to reduce the causes of global warming. This was later confirmed at Kyoto 1998 with the agreements on targets for reducing carbon dioxide emissions. The target for Britain was a reduction of 15 per cent by 2015. Both sets of targets will create external pressure on freight transport to implement appropriate solutions.

A part of the solution will come from research commissioned by DETR through Heriot Watt university to identify a small family of key performance indicators (KPIs) that link freight operational performance with environmental impact. Traditionally, government has used tonnes kilometres as a measure of freight activity. This particular ratio, however, is not a key driver of operational efficiency. The work conducted with industry has identified five KPIs that

influence the transport business and the trends in freight performance and its impact on the environment. The five ratios are: time
utilization, space utilization, empty running, predictability, and
miles per gallon. The work has started in the temperature-controlled sector and will extend to other sectors. The end result will
be an industry-based measurement that both drives efficiency and
demonstrates environmental benefit.

Another part of the solution will be a review of city logistics to
reduce traffic congestion, improve air quality and, where practical,
consolidate part loads into fuller loads for inner urban deliveries.
One option is to deliver during the night but that requires a solution to the major issue of noise and residents. Whatever is done in
this area needs to be realistic and practical. There is some experience from the continent where cities protect their inner core.

Technology

In 1997 Tesco gave a commitment to share information with its suppliers. They could have the information they wanted; in return,
Tesco wanted them to dedicate resources to focus on Tesco customer wishes and then provide appropriate product offerings. This
commitment complemented the change in commercial structure to
focus on category management. Tesco wanted to move on from the
traditional single point of contact with suppliers between the buyer
and the national account manager to a more complex interaction
with suppliers in which different functions worked together. This
commitment to share information required system support to give
the visibility of the same information to both Tesco commercial
teams and their supplier teams. Tesco set up a strategic development
with GE Information to create a commercially secure data exchange
system based on Internet principles; it was called Tesco Information
Exchange (TIE). A limited number of key suppliers then joined the
pilot phase before a phased roll-out was implemented. Promotion
was a key area identified through Efficient Consumer Response
(ECR) as an opportunity to provide a better offer to the consumer,
a simpler operation to manage at all stages and a cheaper supply

chain cost by avoiding the waste of overstocking or large fluctuations in demands.

Rail

Rail is likely to become more important in freight transport in the next ten years because of the environmental issues discussed earlier. Within the United Kingdom, the rail freight infrastructure is being put in place as an alternative to congested sections of the motorway network for long-haul trunk movements. Within the EU it has been agreed that the opening up of freight freeways should allow rail to become more cost competitive with road and other modes of transport.

Home shopping

Tesco recognized that customers wanted a range of retail formats for their various shopping needs. As well as a variety of sizes and locations such as the edge of town superstore, compact market town store, city metro and fuel-linked express, customers showed an interest in other forms of shopping. Hence, in 1995 Tesco conducted a pilot in home shopping at Osterley Store near Heathrow. Customers could use a variety of methods: telephoning a customer service centre, fax, personal computer with CD ROM or the Internet. A menu-style screen gave the customer the choice of selection process for shopping, for example, by accessing a product category or new products etc. These orders were then picked at the store by Tesco staff and could be collected or delivered to the customer's home or drop-off point. This pilot was extended to ten stores in the London postcode area in 1997.

The logistics implications of home shopping can develop into a range of support structures, although it is too early to predict which scenario will become dominant. Whatever the option, home delivery by van will be the principal mode. This van will be designed to load products at different temperatures and some thought has been given to the best environmentally friendly fuel. All stock will be picked at store by retail staff. This would apply where home shopping is a small, even though important, share of shopping in a geographical area. The retail store provides a wider selection of products for consumer selection than any single distribution centre since these are specialized for specific ranges of product. A warehouse look-alike shop set up solely for picking customers' orders could apply in a population of high home shopping density. Such a facility could be built at lower cost in a warehouse-type location.

CONCLUSION

The aim of this chapter was to understand and account for the changes in physical distribution in food retailing by examining changes both in general and in one company, Tesco, in particular. The basic premise is that the transformation in retailing that the food consumer sees has been supported by a transformation in distribution methods and practices. In particular, there has been an increase in the status and professionalism of distribution as the time costs and implications of the function have been recognized. Professionalism has been enhanced by the transformation of distribution through the application of modern methods and technology. Whether the retailer now focuses on quality or on price, the importance of distribution is undeniable. As retailers have responded to consumer change and moved up-market, so the need to improve the quality of distribution has become paramount. At the price-conscious end of the spectrum, the need for low-cost distribution is fundamental to reducing the operating cost of the business. This is not to say that quality retailers are not worried about costs or that discount retailers do not care about quality, but in each case there is a guiding strategy from the business that conditions the strategy of distribution.

The Tesco study demonstrates many aspects of this transformation. In response to the clear business strategy that emerged in the 1970s, 1980s and 1990s, distribution strategy has been realigned. From a state of almost decentralization and poor control, the company has moved to centralization and then composites which have enabled control to be exercised stringently and have led to new methods and relationships for distribution. This is summarized in Table 8.3 which, while based on the changes in Tesco distribution in the 1980s, uses the structure of the distribution in this time. These may be summarized as new benchmarks for stocking policy and locations; new distribution centre operations and systems; widespread use of technology; new material handling systems; and different management structures involving specialist distribution contractors.

The development outlined above and the transformation described are not the ultimate solution. As consumers change their needs, so retailing must and will respond. As retailing responds, companies will modify their operations, not least their distribution, or be placed at a competitive disadvantage. The pursuit of increased control described in this chapter has been enabled by technology. Control by information has replaced control by 'doing'. Another factor has been co-operation with suppliers rather than confrontation, as in the past. In other areas of distribution, change can be contemplated or considered. This situation in distribution is a changing one. Focusing solely on the retail outlet conceals many of the fundamental business changes that have occurred and will continue to occur as shopping behaviour changes.

DISCLAIMER

The views and opinions expressed in this chapter are strictly personal and must not be taken as a statement of policy at Tesco Stores Ltd.

REFERENCES

Akehurst, G (1984) Checkout: the analysis of oligopolistic behaviour in the UK grocery retail market, *Service Industries Journal*, 4(2), pp 198–242
Belussi, F (1987) Benetton: information technology in production and distribution, *SPRU Occasional Paper Number 25*, University of Sussex
Christopher, M (1997) *Marketing Logistics*, Butterworth-Heinemann, Oxford

Table 8.3 Distribution changes in Tesco in 1980s and 1990s

	Features
storage facilities	centralized control
	specialized depots (bonds/fast-moving)
	composite
	in-house and contractor management
	site location and scale
	owned premises
	two picking methods
	increased product range
inventory management	bar coding
	date coding
	fewer investment buys
	reduced stock holding
	quality control
	service levels
	fresh foods
	reduced stock holding
	own fleet
	bigger trailers, less deliveries
	supplier collections
transport	delivery window targets
	multi-temperature trailers
	primary distribution
unitization	pallets, roll cages, dollies
	plastic trays
	pack sizes for merchandising
	pre-packs
communications	computerized systems
	e-mail
	electronic data interchange
	sales-based order
	depot on-line real-time systems
	forecasting
	checkout plus
	hand-held scanners with radio
	frequency

Corina, M (1971) *Pile It High, Sell It Cheap*, Weidenfeld & Nicolson, London

Dawson, JA and Sparks, L (1985) *Issues in Retailing*, Scottish Development Department, Edinburgh

Edwards, C and Gray, M (1990) Tesco case study, in *Electronic Trading*, ed Department of Trade and Industry, HMSO, London

Fernie, J (ed) (1990) *Retail Distribution Management*, Kogan Page, London

Fernie, J (1997) Retail change and retail logistics in the UK: past trends and future prospects, *Service Industries Journal*, 17(3), pp 383–96

Gardner, C and Sheppard, J (1989) *Consuming Passion: The Rise of Retail Culture*, Unwin Hyman, London

Gattorna, JL and Walters, DW (1996) *Managing the Supply Chain: A Strategic Perspective*, Macmillan, Basingstoke

Hendry, M (1995) *Improving Retail Efficiency through EDI: Managing the Supply Chain*, FT Management Report, Pearson, London

INS (1991) *Tesco: Breaking Down the Barriers of Trade*, INS, Sunbury-on-Thames

Kirkwood, DA (1984a) The supermarket challenge, *Focus on PDM*, 3(4), pp 8–12

Kirkwood, DA (1984b) How Tesco manage the distribution function, *Retail and Distribution Management*, 12(5), pp 61–5

McKinnon, AC (1989) *Physical Distribution Systems*, Routledge, London

McKinnon, AC (1990) Electronic data interchange in the retail supply chain, *International Journal of Retail and Distribution Management*, 18(2), pp 39–42

Powell, D (1991) *Counter Revolution: The Tesco Story*, Grafton Books, London

Senker, J (1989) Food retailing, technology and its relation to competitive strategy, in *Technology Strategy and the Firm*, ed M. Dodgson, pp 134–44, Longman, Oxford

Smith, DLG and Sparks, L (1993) The transformation of physical distribution in retailing: the example of Tesco plc, *The International Review of Retail, Distribution and Consumer Research*, 3(1), pp 35–64

Sparks, L (1986) The changing structure of distribution in retail companies, *Transactions of the Institute of British Geographers*, 11(2), pp 147–54

Sparks, L (1988) Technological change and spatial change in UK retail distribution, in *Transport Technology and Spatial Change*, ed RS Tolley, pp 123–48, Institute of British Geographers, North Staffordshire Polytechnic

Walsh, JP (1991) The social context of technological change: the case of the retail food industry, *The Sociological Quarterly*, 32, pp 447–68

Walters, DW (1988) *Strategic Retailing Management*, Prentice-Hall, Hemel Hempstead

9

RESPONDING TO THE CHALLENGES: THE CASE OF SAFEWAY

Lawrence Christensen

INTRODUCTION

This chapter outlines a practical example of how the supply chain can be used to gain competitive advantage. Safeway is a major UK grocery retailer, employing over 66 000 staff, and concentrating on the home market with over 450 stores of an average size of 30 000 sq. ft. Annual sales are £7.1 billion and there was an operating profit of £430 million for the year ended 31 March 1997.

The key corporate objectives are, first, to increase value to the shareholders through the Customer Proposition – which is making shopping easier for today's families, and, second, innovation, particularly in the use of technology, with such things as self-scanning equipment for use by loyalty card holders shopping in store.

SAFEWAY'S LOGISTICS DIVISION

The obvious objective of the Logistics Division is to ensure that it supports the Customer Proposition by improving availability and increasing freshness and constantly to strive to improve operational effectiveness by supporting business expansion, developing flexibility, increasing cost efficiency and reducing wastage.

The Logistics Division is made up of two main operational functions ie distribution operations and supply chain operations (see Figure 9.1). The structure consists of a Logistics Director, supported by the following functions:

- supply chain operations;
- distribution operations;
- human resources support team;
- financial support team;
- strategy and central support services.

Supply chain operations

Supply chain operations is the team responsible for controlling the flow of product through the supply chain to ensure that the correct

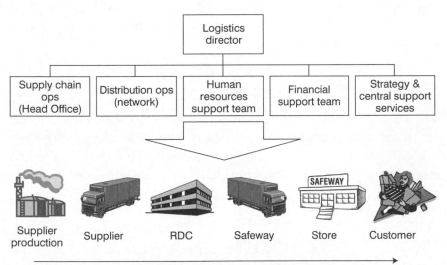

Figure 9.1 Safeway logistics organization chart.

amount of product is brought in at exactly the right time to ensure minimum wastage or wasted working capital with maximum availability on shelf in store at all times.

Distribution operations

Distribution operations is the network of distribution centres and the associated transport operations that handle the product within the supply chain to the stores.

Human resources support team

People are an important part of the Logistics Division and there is a human resources support team in place to ensure that full training and employment packages are provided.

Financial support team

Obviously, monitoring of performance is important and the financial support team ensure that this happens by assisting and monitoring key performance data as well as controlling the normal financial accounting process.

Strategy and central support services

The strategy and central support services team assist in the constant strive for new thinking and new ideas as well as continually keeping current systems and processes updated. This enables the efficient control of the total supply chain as a single process from the factory to the customer.

THE LOGISTICS NETWORK

The Logistics Division handles 9 million cases of output per week, over 22 000 products; 98 per cent of the goods that a Safeway supermarket sells are handled through the distribution network. There are 2 500 suppliers delivering into the Safeway network, with 11 800 orders placed every week. There are 3 million sq. ft. of warehousing, with 4 500 people employed within the division, and the division operates nearly 700 tractor units and over 1 000 trailers. The fleet covers over 100 million kilometres per annum, with an annual fuel bill of around £18 million.

The distribution network consists of 12 distribution centres (see Figure 9.2). However, the backbone of the network is the five big composite warehouses at Bellshill, Stockton, Warrington, Bristol and Aylesford. They are supported by the remaining distribution centres, especially by the central hub at Tamworth in Staffordshire, which handles all the medium-moving and slow-moving products for England and Wales.

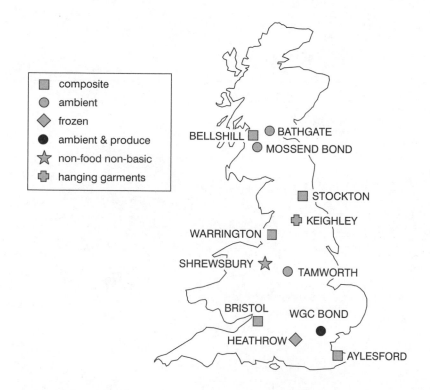

Figure 9.2 Safeway distribution network, February 1998

Roughly 60 per cent of the products handled are ambient, with the remainder falling into the categories of perishable (meat and dairy products) produce and frozen foods (see Figure 9.3). Within the ambient area, volume splits down into the main categories of fast-moving grocery, medium-moving grocery, tobacco, wines and spirits and non-food/non-basic such as children's clothing.

Figure 9.4 illustrates the importance of the large composite distribution centres. Some 72 per cent of volume is handled through these centres, and with the volume of the central hub at Tamworth added, the total percentage handled is 88 per cent.

Safeway is a firm believer in the use of third parties: 39 per cent of volume handled through the network is handled through third

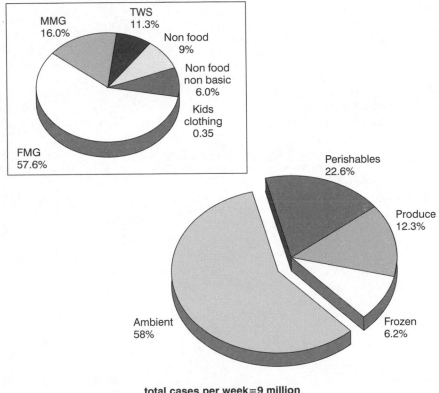

total cases per week=9 million

Figure 9.3 Safeway product mix total division

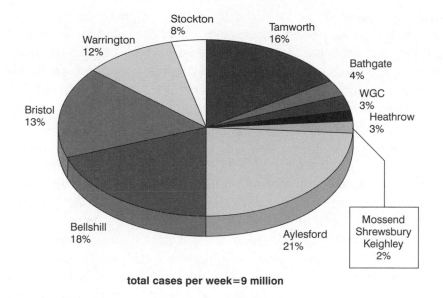

total cases per week=9 million

Figure 9.4 Safeway weekly output mix total division

party depots, where the employees are employed by third party contractors such as Exel Logistics, Wincanton, Christian Salvesen, and Transport Development Group. All the assets, in the main, are still owned by Safeway.

KEY ACHIEVEMENTS TO DATE

The key achievements made by the Logistics Division since the acquisition of Safeway have been in the area of centralized distribution. Where originally only 26 per cent of the volume delivered to stores was handled through the central distribution network, the percentage has risen to its current 98 per cent. This has involved the building of new state-of-the-art facilities and the investment of many millions of pounds in the distribution network.

Within the supply chain, the introduction of sales-based ordering and heavy investment by the company in information technology mean that the re-ordering of product is now almost totally automated and starts from the scanning equipment in the store. Every time a customer purchases a product, the information related to that sale passes back up the supply chain to the supplier to regenerate a new order. The central supply teams are constantly monitoring this information to ensure that the correct volumes are processed through the supply chain and take into account such things as weather changes and promotional activity.

Significant progress has been made from the old adversarial approach to purchasing products towards building supplier partnerships, where suppliers and retailers together examine every aspect of their relationship, including logistics, to find the best way to reduce costs and optimize supply to mutual advantage.

Electronic Data Interchange (EDI) is now used on over 70 per cent of the orders placed with suppliers and its development is seen as having a significant role in improving efficiencies in the supply chain in areas such as green lane receiving[1] and the exchange of information on supply problems, and in payment of invoices. It further facilitates the resolution of issues and speeds up the supply process.

Line picking fresh foods is now a standard fresh food operation within Safeway and this method of operation has enabled a full day's life to be added to the freshest of products, such as pre-packed salad, sandwiches and cream cakes, which has significantly improved the freshness to the customer and reduced wastage to the company.

Central restructure

The company now operates its trading division in the form of business units, with each unit responsible for a number of products. The supply chain teams at the centre mirror the business units and actually work within them, thus giving a totally integrated approach to supply. This is seen as the first step towards category management whereby product categories will be managed by cross-functional teams with total 'bottom line' responsibility.

Achievements within the distribution network include network rationalization, where the many distribution centres have been reduced to the 12 currently in operation, and warehouse technology, including such aspects as radio frequency, receiving, labour management systems, and warehouse management systems.

Backhauling

Backhauling was pioneered by Safeway in the United Kingdom. This is where delivery is made to the store and then the vehicle on the way back to the distribution centre will collect products from the supplier and return them to the mainstream distribution centre.

Networking

In the past, scheduling of transport was a 'local' activity from distribution centre to stores within its catchment area. Now the transport fleet is managed on a national basis whereby Safeway vehicles deliver to stores then pick up from suppliers and/or Tamworth or one of the specialist depots before returning to one of the five composites.

Satellite tracking

Safeway's satellite tracking and driver management system has shown significant improvements in fuel utilization, reduction in delays at stores and general improvements in transport efficiency. Savings of several million of pounds per year have been made through the implementation of this system. The system allows drivers and depots to communicate more effortlessly, thereby alerting drivers to road congestion spots. Also, stores are informed when a vehicle arrival is imminent to confirm schedule windows.

Single items

Over 3 000 lines are picked as single items in the Safeway network at a distribution centre at Shrewsbury. This has meant significant reductions in working capital and overall efficiency improvements within the supply chain.

SUMMARY OF ACHIEVEMENTS

During the past five-year period of dramatic change and rationalization, the business has also continued to grow quickly; range has increased by 37 per cent and volumes by over 40 per cent; off-shore activity in the Scottish Islands, the Isle of Man and the Channel Islands have all increased. Case output per sq. ft. has increased by 50 per cent and all key performance indicators (KPIs) on all service measures have improved significantly. At the same time, cost as a percentage of sales has reduced by 0.7 per cent. This represents a saving in the region of £40 million in distribution costs. However, one other major achievement of the Logistics Division has been its approach to the environment. It has pioneered recycling plants for use of returnable packaging (RTP) backhaul, nitrogen gas, refrigerated trailers, even vehicle washers using waste water from roof drains and refrigeration plants.

SUPPLY CHAIN 2000

Looking to the future of the supply chain after the millennium, the expanding business and increasing customer expectations will require either an increase in costs or a complete rethinking in supply chain methods. The last such revolution took place when products were moved from direct to central supply. This central supply network is now being squeezed to the point where the level of efficiency to be gained is beginning to level out (see Figure 9.5). We therefore need to find a new way forward. That new way forward is called continuous replenishment.

Continuous replenishment

Continuous replenishment means that products never stop, are never stored. This means reduction in waste, reduction in working capital being tied up unnecessarily, general improvement in overall efficiency and a flow through process right from the supplier to the

BUT – there is a limit to how far you can improve availability without a 'step change' in the way the Supply Chain is managed

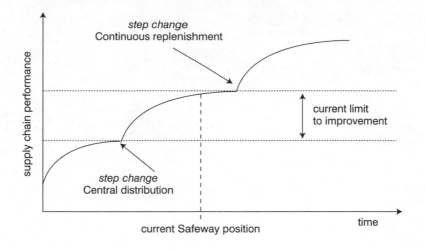

Figure 9.5 Safeway Supply Chain 2000

store. It also means that different channels of distribution can be used such as direct delivery, consolidation centres, straight from production operations to store. This also requires an evaluation process to ensure that products go down the right channel, at the right time (see Figure 9.6).

Fresh food

There will be an increased focus on freshness and therefore a need to speed up products in the supply chain. One of the ways in which the fresh supply chain can operate more efficiently is through fresh consolidation centres. A lot of produce is imported into the country, and also products which are brought into distribution centres from the growing areas involve the use of middle men and suppliers delivering direct to distribution centres.

A consolidation point upstream of the main distribution centre means that company buyers can buy products directly into the

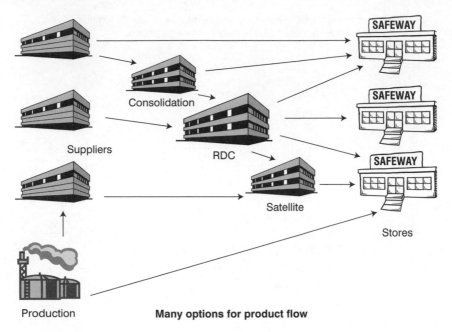

Figure 9.6 Flow through supply chain

consolidation point and then send very efficient loads into the distribution centres, thus making productivity gains in the mainstream composite warehouses and cutting out the costs of middle men.

Factory gate pricing

Factory gate pricing is another concept for the future, whereby the supplier will not have to worry about the price of delivery from factory to the distribution centre. Retailers will take control of this aspect of the supply chain and will use their skill to create a supply chain transport network which, again, squeezes significant costs out of the overall network. By using computerized vehicle routes and scheduling systems in the warehouse, automation and sortation systems will come more and more to the fore as packaging becomes more standardized.

Single item picking

Single item picking will increase as ranges increase in store. This will also allow for the impact of home delivery and the effect of other methods of supplying the consumer to take effect.

Transport optimization

Transport optimization will continue to grow through use of back-haul techniques and supplier deliveries to store together with over-laying of other companies' networks. Perhaps in the future, there will just be a fleet of white lorries delivering from the supplier to the distribution centre and from the distribution centre to Sainsbury, Tesco, Asda and Safeway stores.

Ambient and frozen consolidation

Ambient consolidation warehousing is a relatively new phenomenon whereby mainly slower-moving products from several suppliers are consolidated upstream of the mainstream warehouse, thus enabling efficient use of transport on a 'just-in-time' basis into the main Regional Distribution Centre and allowing line pick to zero or cross-dock to occur. At the same time this allows suppliers to deliver to less stockholding points and to optimize their production runs.

The use of rail, particularly on in-bound freight, will grow significantly over the next five years. Technology will further enhance the effectiveness of the supply chain by creating real-time stock files in stores, thus taking significant chunks of time out of the system and the use of shelf-edge computing for store stock checks will significantly improve accuracy.

Category management

Category management is the next big step forward. This broadly means that the company's product range is broken down into logical categories for which one cross-functional team is responsible to ensure that the net profit of that category is optimized. Supply Chain 2000 and distribution operations will therefore be an inherent part of the trading operation to ensure that the optimum solution is achieved for the total supply chain of each category.

CONCLUSIONS

This chapter has shown how one company, Safeway Stores plc, has managed its supply chain since the acquisition of Safeway by the Argyll Group over a decade ago. The first step change was the move to centralization from 26 per cent of volume delivered to 98 per cent. The distribution network has been rationalized and considerable investment has been channelled into new state-of-the-art facilities and systems technology. This has paid off in terms of results; in the last five years, volumes have increased by 40 per cent yet costs as a percentage of sales have fallen by 0.7 per cent.

The challenges for the future are demanding. It is unlikely that any more costs can be squeezed out of the supply chain unless another step change in management philosophy is forthcoming. In Supply Chain 2000, Safeway intend to make that step change through the use of category management and continuous replenishment techniques. Greater flexibility will be required in managing the flow of product from factory to store in that different channels of distribution will be used to ensure optimization of warehouse and transport resources.

[1] Where Safeway has EDI links with suppliers, they receive priority at distribution centres for the off-loading of their products.

10

THE DEVELOPMENT OF RETAIL SUPPORT SERVICES

John O'Hagan

INTRODUCTION

The explosive growth of the major retail chains during the 1980s was mirrored by an equally explosive investment in distribution systems. Taking as their model just-in-time supply chain management developed originally by the motor industry, the retail groups have developed sophisticated networks dedicated to making sure that merchandise is distributed between suppliers and outlets in the most cost-efficient way possible.

Distribution managers of the 1970s would not recognize the systems and methods of today. From manufacturers and suppliers delivering products direct to stores, retailers have almost universally embraced the concept of central distribution from owned or third-party managed depots. Equipment manufacturers have assisted, with the development of multi-ambient warehouses, trucks and trailers for the grocery industry and specialized transport and storage for other types of retail merchandise, such as hanging garments.

Although distribution systems differ from group to group, they all have the ultimate objective of enhancing profit margins, and hence profits, by improving the efficiency of the supply chain. By cutting costs, improving productivity and maximizing sales per square foot through the elimination of wasted space, the traditionally high operational gearing of the retail industry means that incremental improvements in individual cost areas can have a significant effect on profits.

In particular, we shall look at what Hays has done in this area of retail management.

EXTENDING THE CONCEPT

Ask any retail operations director how much their centralized distribution system costs (and how much it saves) and they will tell you down to the last penny. But how many could say how much they spend storing, transporting and managing non-merchandise items – those diverse items from tills to displays that are needed to support every retail operation? Perhaps even more important, how many have given serious thought to how much valuable retail space these items can take up at each store – space that could be used to generate more sales?

Despite the vast sums spent developing merchandise distribution systems, there are still relatively few organizations – whether retailers or other multi-site high street operators such as banks, building societies, estate agents or travel agents – that apply the same professional disciplines to their retail support items. Shopfittings, uniforms, stationery, IT equipment, shopping trolleys and consumables are all essential to high street trading yet little control is exercised over their storage, refurbishment or even transfer between units.

Imagine a supermarket chain of 100 outlets where each local manager is responsible for his or her own retail support operation. Suddenly there are 100 storerooms to control, each carrying duplicate stocks of what are often expensive items. One manager might easily order new display shelving, for example, when it is surplus to requirements, probably gathering dust, at another store in the group.

There are 100 opportunities for goods to become damaged, lost, allowed to lie idle or even be discarded unnecessarily. Savings fought for by those involved centrally in the purchase of such items are lost.

A NEW STORE AT NO COST

But before the cost savings from improved inventory control are taken into account, what retailer would turn down the opportunity to add an extra store to the network for free? By keeping stock levels to a minimum, additional space will be released in each store. If sales space can be increased by just 1 per cent at each of those 100 supermarkets, the equivalent of a whole new store is created at no capital cost whatsoever.

Better inventory control

In terms of inventory control, let's look at one specific product – staff uniforms might seem a trivial item to focus upon but they highlight the cost benefit of centralization perfectly. Many retailers keep stocks of all sizes in each outlet, thereby holding numbers well in excess of actual requirements. Consider the savings to be made by storing them in a single central location. In Hays' experience, stocks held in reserve can generally be cut by three-quarters, at a stroke. The appropriate sizes required by each store can be ordered and delivered along with regular orders of other support items. Uniforms returned by staff to the centre can be cleaned, repaired and stored, thus relieving the outlet of an extra task, whilst reducing cost. Any finance director looking at the cost of uniforms throughout the year will be able to calculate the savings if he is able to reduce average stock levels by 75 per cent. The benefits will be equally obvious to any purchasing executive.

While possible cost savings from centralized storage and distribution of each type of item on its own may look relatively insignificant, the real benefit comes when the complete range of retail support products are taken together. Display shelves, racking, shopping trolleys, tills, stationery, mannequins, window displays, training resources, mobile equipment for merchandise, office and staff quarters furniture, photocopiers, fax machines, computers, fire extinguishers and stockroom items are all candidates for similar treatment.

Greater management control

The benefits of centralized warehousing and distribution of non-merchandise items extend much further than stock reduction. Retailers will gain greater control over a wider range of goods while reducing the amount of management time involved – both at head office and individual store levels.

Inventory management systems to handle retail support items need to operate in a similar fashion to those for merchandise, in that they should consolidate all the goods in one central or a small number of locations. Centralization inevitably cuts down on the amount of stock needed, thereby reducing working capital requirements, which could be used on new store openings, displays, IT etc.

The economies of scale which centralization brings allow full use to be made of specialist handling systems and specially trained staff to ensure efficient picking/stock replenishment. At the same time it significantly reduces the risk of costly damages and product deterioration.

The importance of IT

To work effectively, central inventory control of retail support items does of course need sophisticated IT systems, which in turn calls for sound management and substantial investment by the service provider. Ideally, such systems should have on-line links to customers and provide instant access to the location of every support product and its asset value so that existing resources can be used as efficiently as possible. Automated or semi-automated ordering procedures, direct links to accounts systems and detailed management reports will also help to ensure that management time is better utilized and operational costs are reduced.

Refurbishment

The useful life of many retail support items is unnecessarily shortened because individual branches or outlets do not have the resources to make repairs or are unaware of the requirements of other branches, which may be able to use their surplus items. Many fittings are changed due to seasonal merchandising requirements or site refurbishment; however, their life can be extended by managing and controlling stocks effectively.

Cleaning, rebuilding, varnishing, veneering, powder coating and zinc plating are just some of the methods used to give fittings a new lease of life. The experience of organizations taking the centralization route is that up to 50 per cent of shopfittings can be salvaged, refurbished and then either returned to the original outlet or put into Hays' computerized store until required for use in another location. Any repairs or modifications required for the new store can be carried out off-site prior to delivery. Again, savings on expenditure on fixtures and fittings will fall straight to the bottom line.

The underlying factor of any refurbishment work is the quality of the finished product – it has to be as new. Nowhere is this more important than in the highly specialized area of refrigeration cabinets, where refurbishment might entail replacing as much as 70 per cent of the unit – even so, it is still a significant saving on new.

Used cabinets will be stripped right down to the carcass before being rewired and repiped with whatever type of defrost and case controllers the customer requires. All external and internal panels are replaced, and any new merchandising equipment supplied as required. Electrical circuits will be replaced and flash tested, and coils pressure tested.

HAYS PROJECT MANAGEMENT

It has been a natural progression for Hays to move into the related areas of project managing as well as physically undertaking store installations, refurbishments and refits. For a new store opening,

Hays offers complete management control of all aspects relating to the fitting out. The company employs qualified surveyors, project managers, co-ordinators and supervisors who will discuss layouts with clients to ensure items are installed in the most efficient and cost-effective way.

All retail support items will be collected, consolidated and quality inspected at a central point. Damaged or missing items, which could cause expensive delays if not noticed until the project has started, can be dealt with more easily. As much pre-assembly work will be carried out as possible to reduce installation time. Delivery to site is then phased in line with the client's schedule. Like merchandise, it can be delivered 'just-in-time' for installation – saving the need for on-site storage and management of items arriving at different times from different suppliers.

While installing modern display equipment may no longer need the expertise of expensive shopfitting professionals, it still needs specialist handling. Hays provides installation teams trained in the handling and assembly of all types of shopfitting equipment, so retailers can call on one company for delivery and fitting, saving both time and money.

Hays can undertake minor or major shop refurbishment – dismantling and removing fittings, undertaking building maintenance, decorating, joinery, ceiling or floor installation, before delivering and installing new or refurbished equipment. For refits carried out while a store is trading, Hays will work overnight or at the weekend, completing a section at a time so no trading time is lost. Teams will move in at closing time, de-merchandise displays, undertake any layout/equipment changes and then re-merchandise in time for the store opening next day. The installation of special promotional equipment or signage can also be undertaken overnight.

Should an outlet have to close, Hays will undertake the dismantling and removal of all items, including carpets and awkward objects such as safes. These can then be sorted, refurbished, disposed of or put into store at Hays' or the client's warehouse for use elsewhere.

In-bound supply

Hays is beginning to forge much closer links with suppliers of retail support products. There is further scope for improving efficiency by exerting greater control of the in-bound supply chain – ideally sitting round the table with suppliers and the retailer at the planning stage of a new store. Savings can be achieved in areas of packaging and handling, production runs can be planned more effectively and transport costs can be minimized if collection and delivery days are arranged taking into account Hays' fleet availability. In other words, analysing the supply chain as a whole from beginning to end; recognizing that the chain has to be balanced. The most economic option for one link in the chain might not lead to the most cost-effective solution overall.

Asset management

Centralized, computerized inventory provides retailers with the ability to financially manage their assets far more effectively. Currently Hays catalogues large items with an individual asset number, monitoring movements in and out and allowing complete traceability. By attaching an asset value to each item, retailers are able to monitor the total value of retail support products at each store and charge the stores according to their usage. As soon as stores see that they are being charged in this way, there is a much greater incentive both to look after the equipment more carefully and to return surplus equipment as soon as possible to remove it from their asset register.

CASE STUDIES

M & S – a pioneer

Marks & Spencer, a pioneer in many areas of retailing, was the first retailer to recognize the potential benefits of applying professional logistics skills to retail support services. The company's relationship with Hays Retail Support Services (known until 1995 as Bucks) dates back over 30 years. Today, Marks & Spencer uses the facilities of Hays for the centralized management of all its sales floor and backstage equipment in the same way that many other retailers use third parties to handle their retail products.

Marks & Spencer's refurbishment of its flagship Marble Arch store serves as a useful case study of the benefits of centralized management of store fittings. All the refurbishment components were manufactured almost 400 miles from the store. Hays co-ordinated the transportation of goods to one of its own ware-houses in London for consolidation, where shopfitters carried out the pre-assembly of units by day prior to installation at night. At Marble Arch, merchandise was cleared and old shelves and dis-plays removed by Hays each evening after closing. The new part-assembled units were transported to the store, positioned and fitted, then the merchandise sorted and re-merchandised on the new counters ready for trading the following day. Not a minute's trading was lost. In addition, the old equipment was taken to Hays' central warehouse to be dismantled into components before passing through a vigorous quality control system which ear-marked every item for disposal, refurbishment or storage for future use elsewhere. The advantage to Marks & Spencer of the centralized logistical support was quickly apparent. Without it, local storage space would have needed sourcing for the new equipment prior to installation, and Marks & Spencer's own staff would probably have removed and replaced merchandise, thus adding overtime costs to the overall bill.

IKEA

Centralizing its store fittings operation with Hays Retail Support Services gave Swedish home furnishing giant IKEA an immediate benefit – a saving of almost 30 per cent of the cost of new display equipment for its next store refurbishment. The saving was achieved following a fixtures and fittings sortation exercise carried out by Hays to retrieve surplus stock held at each of the company's massive retail operations spread throughout the United Kingdom. Almost 500 pallets of mixed equipment, including shelving, uprights and display mesh were brought into Retail Support Services' centralized warehouse near Derby, where it was sorted, computer logged and held in specialist racking designed to cope with these large and difficult-to-store items. The inventory of display equipment required for the refurbishment of IKEA's Warrington store was then passed to the warehouse prior to any new items being ordered. Retail Support Services was able to fulfil almost 30 per cent of the inventory from stock held in store.

IKEA is tied to Swedish suppliers for its store equipment, which involves added problems of lead times, handling and shipping, with goods sometimes having to be ordered before exact requirements are known. Over the years, local managers had developed a tendency to add 10 per cent to their orders to avoid potential problems. Slowly this led to an accumulation of stock, taking up space in each outlet but not being properly stored, so it was becoming damaged. By centralizing storage of fixtures and fittings IKEA saved the annual cost of the operation in one single exercise. In addition to saving on new equipment, it has also saved on damages and freed up valuable space at each store for retail use. Each IKEA store now receives a monthly inventory of fixtures and fittings in stock which it can obtain direct from Hays, while orders for new items are still handled by IKEA's UK head office.

A successful amnesty

An existing Hays client was planning an extensive programme of store refurbishments. Although already managing a dedicated warehouse for the retailer, where all surplus shopfittings and equipment were stored, Hays, as part of its customer care programme, proposed undertaking surveys of a number of stores to ascertain whether additional fittings were being held in stockrooms or warehouses. The results were startling. Millions of pounds' worth of equipment was found that would have remained under-utilized. As a result, the client issued an 'Amnesty' note to all 200 stores and

Hays eventually collected and inspected over 1000 pallet loads of shelves, brackets and displays.

Sainsbury's

January 1997 saw Sainsbury's become the first food retailer to centralize its retail support operations with Hays. The retailer has given Hays responsibility for stock centralization, specialist transportation and on-site installation of all its shop fittings and display equipment for the next five years. Sainsbury's was using numerous manufacturers and shopfitting companies to carry out these operations but an in-depth assessment exercise by Hays demonstrated the clear benefits of centralization.

For Sainsbury's Hays has collected and centralized all surplus equipment from branches throughout the country. This has given the retailer a complete inventory of all items, thereby eliminating the unnecessary purchase of new equipment and keeping stock-holding to a minimum. Distribution of goods to over 350 Sainsbury's stores through Hays' shared-user delivery option is bringing further financial advantages to the food retailer. In addition, Hays is instigating a refurbishment programme to ensure all items achieve full life potential. Hays' recent acquisition of refrigeration refurbishment specialists, North and South Installations Ltd., has given Sainsbury's the added benefit of cost-saving refurbishment services for its large number of refrigerated displays which are included in the five-year deal.

INCREASED PROFITS – THE BOTTOM LINE

For these organizations, contracting out retail support operations means much more than improved control of non-merchandise items. Every product carries its own handling and financing costs; savings from consolidation can be as much as 0.15 per cent to 0.25 per cent of turnover (after allowing for the operator's costs), depending on the extent it is applied across the range of non-merchandise items. This may sound small but, translated into profit for a company with a low net margin, it can mean a substantial increase in profits. For example, if an organization with sales of £500 million and a net margin of 3 per cent were to make savings of 0.2 per cent of turnover, its profits would be boosted by £1 million, or 6.25 per cent. Any manager who could achieve savings on that scale would be worth his or her weight in gold.

INDEX

Further reading from Kogan Page

The Transport Manager's and Operator's Handbook 1999 (29th edition)
David Lowe
ISBN 0 7494 2911 9 Paperback

Global Logistics and Distribution Planning (3rd edition)
Edited by Donald Waters
ISBN 0 7494 2779 5 Hardback

International Transport (5th edition)
Rex Faulks
Published in association with the Chartered Institute of Transport
ISBN 0 7494 2832 5 Paperback

Applied Transport Economics (2nd edition)
Stuart Cole
ISBN 0 7494 2303 x Paperback

Logistics: An Integrated Approach (2nd edition)
Bryan Jones and Michael Quale
Edited by David Jessop
ISBN 1 8728 0767 4 Paperback